Quod scriptura, non iubet vetat

The Latin translates, "What is not commanded in scripture, is forbidden:'

On the Cover: Baptists rejoice to hold in common with other evangelicals the main principles of the orthodox Christian faith. However, there are points of difference and these differences are significant. In fact, because these differences arise out of God's revealed will, they are of vital importance. Hence, the barriers of separation between Baptists and others can hardly be considered a trifling matter. To suppose that Baptists are kept apart solely by their views on Baptism or the Lord's Supper is a regrettable misunderstanding. Baptists hold views which distinguish them from Catholics, Congregationalists, Episcopalians, Lutherans, Methodists, Pentecostals, and Presbyterians, and the differences are so great as not only to justify, but to demand, the separate denominational existence of Baptists. Some people think Baptists ought not teach and emphasize their differences but as E.J. Forrester stated in 1893, "Any denomination that has views which justify its separate existence, is bound to promulgate those views. If those views are of sufficient importance to justify a separate existence, they are important enough to create a duty for their promulgation ... the very same reasons which justify the separate existence of any denomination make it the duty of that denomination to teach the distinctive doctrines upon which its separate existence rests." If Baptists have a right to a separate denominational life, it is their duty to propagate their distinctive principles, without which their separate life cannot be justified or maintained.

Many among today's professing Baptists have an agenda to revise the Baptist distinctives and redefine what it means to be a Baptist. Others don't understand why it even matters. The books being reproduced in the *Baptist Distinctives Series* are republished in order that Baptists from the past may state, explain and defend the primary Baptist distinctives as they understood them. It is hoped that this Series will provide a more thorough historical perspective on what it means to be distinctively Baptist.

The Lord Jesus Christ asked, *"And why call ye me, Lord, Lord, and do not the things which I say?"* (Luke 6:46). The immediate context surrounding this question explains what it means to be a true disciple of Christ. Addressing the same issue, Christ's question is meant to show that a confession of discipleship to the Lord Jesus Christ is inconsistent and untrue if it is not accompanied with a corresponding submission to His authoritative commands. Christ's question teaches us that a true recognition of His authority as Lord inevitably includes a submission to the authority of His Word. Hence, with this question Christ has made it forever impossible to separate His authority as King from the authority of His Word. These two principles—the authority of Christ as King and the authority of His Word—are the two most fundamental Baptist distinctives. The first gives rise to the second and out of these two all the other Baptist distinctives emanate. As F.M. Iams wrote in 1894, "Loyalty to Christ as King, manifesting itself in a constant and unswerving obedience to His will as revealed in His written Word, is the real source of all the Baptist distinctives:' In the search for the *primary* Baptist distinctive many have settled on the Lordship of Christ as the most basic distinctive. Strangely, in doing this, some have attempted to separate Christ's Lordship from the authority of Scripture, as if you could embrace Christ's authority without submitting to what He commanded. However, while Christ's Lordship and Kingly authority can be isolated and considered essentially for discussion's sake, we see from Christ's own words in Luke 6:46 that His Lordship is really inseparable from His Word and, with regard to real Christian discipleship, there can be no practical submission to the one without a practical submission to the other.

In the symbol above the Kingly Crown and the Open Bible represent the inseparable truths of Christ's Kingly and Biblical authority. The Crown and Bible graphics are supplemented by three Bible verses (Ecclesiastes 8:4, Matthew 28:18-20, and Luke 6:46) that reiterate and reinforce the inextricable connection between the authority of Christ as King and the authority of His Word. The truths symbolized by these components are further emphasized by the Latin quotation - *quod scriptura, non iubet vetat*— i.e., "What is not commanded in scripture, is forbidden:' This Latin quote has been considered historically as a summary statement of the regulative principle of Scripture. Together these various symbolic components converge to exhibit the two most foundational Baptist Distinctives out of which all the other Baptist Distinctives arise. Consequently, we have chosen this composite symbol as a logo to represent the primary truths set forth in the *Baptist Distinctives Series*.

LECTURES
ON
BAPTISM

LECTURES ON BAPTISM

BY THE LATE

WILLIAM SHIRREFF,

Minister of the Gospel, Glasgow

With a Biographical Sketch of the Author by John Franklin Jones

INCLUDING A

PREFACE BY C.H. SPURGEON.

LONDON:
PASSMORE AND ALABASTER,
PATERNOSTER BUILDINGS.
1878

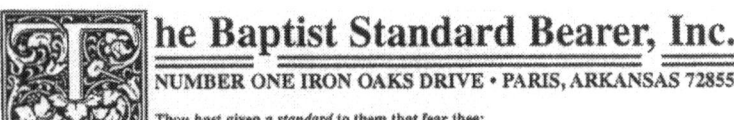

Reprinted 2006

by

THE BAPTIST STANDARD BEARER, INC.
No. 1 Iron Oaks Drive
Paris, Arkansas 72855
(479) 963-3831

THE WALDENSIAN EMBLEM
lux lucet in tenebris
"The Light Shineth in the Darkness"

ISBN# 1579785018

Publisher's Foreword

"I know of no surer way of a people's perishing than by being led by one who does not speak out straight, and honestly denounce evil. If the minister halts between two opinions, do you wonder that the congregation is undecided? If the preacher trims and twists to please all parties, can you expect his people to be honest? If I wink at your inconsistencies will you not soon be hardened in them? Like priest, like people. A cowardly preacher suits hardened sinners. Those who are afraid to rebuke sin, or to probe the conscience, will have much to answer for.... And yet is not a mingle-mangle of Christ and Belial the common religion of the day? Is not worldly piety or pious worldliness the current religion? ...such seek out a trimming teacher who is not too precise and plain spoken, and they settle down comfortably to a mongrel faith, half truth, half error and a mongrel worship half dead form and half orthodoxy.... There can be no alliance between the two... 'No man can serve two masters.' All attempts at compromise or comprehensiveness in matters of truth and purity are founded upon falsehood, and falsehood is all that can come of them. May God save us from such hateful double-mindedness." *Metropolitan Tabernacle Pulpit*, Vol.27 (Pasadena, Texas, Pilgrim Pub., 1973), p. 562.

It is our intention to "speak out straight" and be as "precise and plain spoken" in our Publisher's Forewords as both candor and conviction will allow. That this book will "start" Christians arguing about infant baptism, we deny. The fact is, they already argue about it, and have done so for centuries. Should this book provoke more controversy, we shall not be upset, as long as it is conducted in the proper Christian spirit of meekness and love, in the interest of truth, and for the glory of God. Controversy marks the presence of deep convictions and therefore, usually, thinking minds. If controversy sets men searching the Scriptures, it is by no means a bad thing.

We do not expect to convince everyone who considers the arguments contained in the following book by Mr. William Shirreff, however we categorically declare that this is our hope and our aim. If we did not seek to convince others of what we, as Baptists, believe, it would indicate that we are not fully persuaded and committed ourselves. Since we are convinced that infant baptism is a gross perversion of one of the ordinances of the Lord Jesus Christ, are we not entitled, yea, rather, is it not our duty to oppose it and forthrightly declare what we consider to be the truth? We are not so vain as to suppose that we have all the light. But we know that every additional witness is useful in a disputed legal case. We wish to strengthen the hands of the rising generation of Baptists by shaping in their minds a standard doctrinal identity and showing them that we have no reason to be ashamed of our opinions. At the same time we wish to give the promoters and defenders of infant baptism (and particularly the more aggressive, conservative, Reformed and Presbyterian people) the witness of a former Presbyterian, in the hopes that they, by the blessing of God, will see that the Scriptural arguments in this matter are not, as they suppose, on their side. One of their own, an Anglican bishop, J.C. Ryle, said: "It is impossible to handle this question without coming into direct collision with the opinions of others. But I hope it is possible to handle it in a kindly and temperate spirit. At any rate it is no use to avoid discussion for fear of offending. Disputed points in theology are never likely to be settled unless men on both sides will say out plainly what they think, and give their reasons for their opinions. To avoid the subject, because it is a controversial one, is neither honest nor wise." *Knots Untied*, c. 5, p.75.

In all honesty, we would not make a brother "an offender for a word" (Is. 29:21). We desire to "walk together" (Amos 3:3) "in truth" (3 Jn. 4) with "all them that love our Lord Jesus Christ in sincerity" (Eph. 6:24), who "rejoiceth in the truth"

PUBLISHER'S FOREWORD

(1 Cor. 13:16), and who have determined in their hearts to "prove all things" and only "hold fast that which is good" (1 Thess. 5:21). On the other hand, we shall call no man master. We hold no man's "person in admiration because of advantage" (Jude 16). We seek not "honor from men" nor "one of another" (Jn. 5:41, 44). If we know anything of ourselves, we desire "truth in the inward parts" (Ps. 51: 6). Therefore, regarding this infant baptism controversy (or any other controversy), God being our Helper, we shall not purchase peace at the expense of truth.

Since the early 1800's, the Baptist people in America, for the most part, have departed from the evangelical theology and ecclesiology of their forefathers. We emphasize that the "majority" of professed Baptists have done this --- certainly not all Baptists, for there is "at this present time also ...a remnant" (Rom. 11:5). In their desire to fulfill the Great Commission, the New School Baptists have plunged deeper and deeper into the labyrinth of Arminianism and Pragmatism. Corrupted alike by the Universal Atonement view of Andrew Fuller and the compassionate — but erroneous — evangelistic zeal of William Carey, Luther Rice and Adoniram Judson, the New School Baptists departed further and further from the "Ancient Landmarks" which their fathers had set (Pr. 22:28); for, while professing and preaching an ecclesiology that demanded a separation between the regenerate and unregenerate in the New Testament Church, they devised and implemented pragmatic practices which guaranteed the very opposite. In disdain for, and opposition to, their more numerous and popular New School counterparts, the Old School Strict Baptists have recoiled more and more into criticism, Antinomianism, and Sandemanianism. Both groups find themselves today in a deplorable and disastrously effete condition doctrinally and practically, and at a loss with regard to defending their distinct identity in controversy.

Since the late 1950's and early 1960's, there has been an upsurge in the interest in, and publication of Puritan theology, for most of which, we might add, we are grateful.

But with the exposure to Puritan theology, there has also come an exposure to Puritan, or Protestant ecclesiology, which basically is the same as Catholic ecclesiology, i.e., both being without Biblical basis; the former is founded upon assumption, the latter upon tradition. With this upsurge in Puritan and Protestant publications, the Protestants have been strengthened, renewed and emboldened. The circumstances with the Baptists have been far otherwise. With the passing of time; the death of the older defenders of the Baptist faith; the liberalizing of the Baptist schools; the decline in availability of the writings of the old Baptist authors upon the public bookshelves, and the negligence in republishing the same; the almost complete turnover to Fullerite Arminianism; the emphasizing of pragmatic methodology and glorification of the American goddess of size and success; the "Ancient Landmarks," or historic distinctives of the Baptist faith, have all but disappeared from public memory. In this situation of the weakening and well-nigh silencing of the witness of Baptist ecclesiology, the Protestants have renewed the ancient controversy between themselves and the Baptists. This is nothing new or strange, for as John Gill points out: "The Paedobaptists are ever restless and uneasy, always endeavouring to maintain and support, if possible, their unscriptural practice of infant-baptism; though it is not other than a pillar of Popery." *Infant Baptism, A Part and Pillar of Popery,* (Boston, 1766). Strengthened by the multiplicity of Protestant publications in the last 25 years and emboldened by the timidity and inadequacy of the present-day Baptist rebuttal, the Protestants have thrust forward their champions, who, assuming their invincibility like Goliath of old, hurl forth slander and reproach, while the Baptists, like the army of Israel, cower down fearfully in their trenches. It appears to those who are ignorant of the issues that this controversy is just a matter of disagreement about the amount of water used in baptism. This is far from the major issues involved.

PUBLISHER'S FOREWORD

As far as we are concerned, the practice of infant baptism in Protestant ecclesiology contains within itself at least the following evident errors and inconsistencies:

(1) a *violation* of the basic laws of hermeneutics and a subtle repudiation of the fundamental principle of the absolute necessity for scriptural warrant, and the final authority of the Scriptures in all matters of faith and practice;

(2) an *invasion* and *usurpation* of the crown rights and sole prerogatives of Christ as the only King and Lawgiver of the New Testament Church;

(3) a *defamation* of the Goodness and Wisdom of the Divine character;

(4) a *confusion* of the Everlasting Covenant of Grace and the Abrahamic Covenant of Circumcision;

(5) a *nullification* of the doctrines of original sin and total depravity/inability;

(6) an *abrogation* of the true nature and evidence of Sovereign saving grace and the doctrine of Regeneration;

(7) an *obliteration* and *perversion* of the proper subject, mode and purpose of New Testament baptism;

(8) a *destruction* of the scripturally-required spiritual nature of Christ's New Testament Church (Jn. 18:36), because there is an amalgamation of the world with the saints, the lost with the saved, the believers with unbelievers, and the regenerate with the unregenerate by means of infant-baptism;

(9) an *association* and *integration* of the spiritual church with the political government, completely unjustified by the New Testament;

(10) a *renunciation* of and *opposition* to true individual liberty of conscience and private judgment.

Publisher's Foreword

Therefore, the practice of infant-baptism annuls the basic theological foundations of Christianity. In a word — "grace is no more grace" (Rom. 11:6). Such obvious errors must be opposed. The differences between us are no minor differences.

In 1821, in the preface to his book entitled, *Lacon*, C.C. Coulton said: "There are three difficulties in authorship [and, we might add, in publishing]:

1. to write anything worth publishing;
2. to find skillful and honest men to print it, and
3. to find sincere, diligent and thoughtful men who will read it."

We believe we have found the first two, in Mr. William Shirreff's book entitled, *Lectures on Baptism* and in our current printer/binder. We look now for the third! Will you, my dear friend who now holds this book in your hand, be a "sincere, diligent and thoughtful man who will read it"? That it may be so, is the prayer of the Publisher. We feel it is important to always remind our readers that we do not necessarily agree with **everything** found in the books we publish. Duty requires that we warn and remind our readers to "prove all things," from the Scriptures and "hold fast that which is good" (1 Thess. 5:21). "Consider what I say; and the Lord give thee understanding in all things" (2 Tim. 2:7).

THE BAPTIST STANDARD BEARER, INC.
(Ps. 60:4,5; Is. 59:19; 62:10-12)
PARIS, ARKANSAS
JULY 28, 2006

CONTENTS.

		Page
INTRODUCTORY LECTURE.	Importance of Positive Institutions, and Observations on the Ordinance of Baptism	1
LECT. II.	Nature of the Evidence required ...	9
LECT. III.	The New Testament the only Rule in regard to the Positive Institutions of the Gospel	19
LECT. IV.	Our Practice must be determined by those Passages of Scripture which more directly treat of the subject of Inquiry...	34
LECT. V.	Positive Proof essential to Worship in Baptism	46
LECT. VI.	Estimate of the Value of Inferential Reasoning on the subject of Baptism	57
LECT VII.	Presumptions against Infant Baptism ...	70
LECT. VIII.	Further Presumptions against Infant Baptism	80
LECT. IX.	Further Presumptions against Infant Baptism	93
LECT. X.	Further Presumptions against Infant Baptism	108
LECT. XI.	Concluding Presumptions against Infant Baptism	126

CONTENTS.

		Page
LECT. XII.	The Baptism of John; its Subjects and Mode	141
LECT. XIII.	Baptism of the Disciples during Christ's Humiliation. The Great Commission	150
LECT. XIV.	Baptism at Pentecost	159
LECT. XV.	Baptism of the Samaritans and of the Ethiopian Eunuch	170
LECT. XVI.	Baptism of Saul of Tarsus, and of the Centurion	183
LECT. XVII.	Baptism of Lydia, and of the Jailor	199
LECT. XVIII.	Baptisms at Corinth, unto Moses, at Ephesus, and at Rome	208
LECT. XIX.	Baptisms in Galatia, at Colosse, and 1 Pet. iii. 18—21	220

PREFATORY MEMOIR.

IT is meet that a memoir of the author should precede these Lectures, but it must of necessity be brief, since no life of him has been written, nor do the magazines of the period contain any information as to his life and work. It is more than 50 years since Mr. Shirreff left the Presbyterian Church and was baptized, and hence there are few surviving personal memories to fall back upon. We are, therefore, unable to do more than arrange the materials kindly furnished by our beloved friend, Miss Mary Shirreff, of Rothesay, who is his only surviving daughter. True daughter is she of the man who left all things for Christ's sake: her memorial abides in the hearts of the members of the Baptist Church in Rothesay, to whom she has long been a mother in Israel. To her suggestion, encouragement, and assistance the republication of these Lectures is due.

From a very careful study of his Lectures we should conclude that Mr. Shirreff was a true gentleman as well as a sincere Christian; a man as far removed from bigotry as from indifference. He appears in his writings to be sensitive but not censorious: a man who would be very scrupulous as to his own conduct, but very generous in his estimate of others. In these Lectures there are no hard words, opprobrious epithets, or cutting taunts. He argues, as we think, most convincingly, and his logic is inexorable, but there is not a drop of bitterness in the whole book. Order is apparent almost to rigidity, and hence there is a measure of repetition; but order is evidently one of the writer's virtues, and is so much a part of the man that he must have his way in it even to an extreme. He is determined carefully to prove all things, and hence he boldly *weighs* those arguments of his opponents which at first sight appear to be conclusive, and when he has them in the scale their apparent force vanishes, and they rise into the air as trifles light as air. God's word was evidently Mr. Shirreff's only law, and he tested everything by it, paying no deference to antiquity, tradition, or ecclesiastical certificate. He felt that he must be on the side of Scripture, even if he stood alone. What it cost him to follow his Lord in baptism he best knew, only it is clear that he never regretted the step, but with unclouded brow and easy conscience pursued his even course till "Well done, good and faithful servant," sounded in his ear.

The Lectures are, to our mind, singularly likely to conciliate and win those who already hold sound views upon the great doctrines of the gospel. They were clearly meant to be an appeal to the author's old friends, the Presbyterians. They are thorough and uncompromising, but, at the same time, calm and judicious. Evidently the track laid down is that which had led the author's own mind to his own definite conclusion, and he is sanguine that others will try the path and reach the same end.

We most of all admire in these Lectures the clear determination of the lecturer to obey the will of the Lord, cost what it may. He never wavers, and never imagines it possible for him to compromise with conscience and evade the force of a text in order to avoid self-sacrifice. He is constructed of such stuff as martyrs are made of, with more of the gentle spirit of "the faithful and true witness" than has usually been seen in self-sacrificing confessors. We see the man so well in his communications that we could almost construct a memoir out of our own perceptions; but we are so little given to speculation that we forbear.

Mr. William Shirreff was born at Coldstream, Berwickshire, in 1762. He was an only child: his parents gave him a good education, and he wisely improved his advantages. He determined to excel, and was unremitting in his application to his lessons, having from his earliest childhood a conscientious desire to do right. On one occasion, failing to win a prize, he went to a gravestone and cried till he was ill, but at the same time he resolved to do better in future. While yet young he was the subject of frequent religious impressions, and he was wont specially to recall the struggles of his heart while he was twelve or thirteen years of age, when hearing one of his parents read in the family extracts from the works of the Puritan divines. How much benefit might accrue to all our families if there were more of such solid reading! At sixteen William Shirreff partook of the Communion in the Scotch Established Church. In his diary he says he was serious then, but relapsed.

At seventeen his father's death brought back his religious impressions, and decided his life-course. After the death of his parents he went to Edinburgh, and underwent a long course of study at the University. He was considered an excellent Greek, Hebrew, and Latin scholar, and attained considerable proficiency in the modern languages; he studied mathematics and the other branches of human learning, but he became most of all interested in divinity. To the end of his life he studied theology so earnestly and profoundly that he richly deserved the reputation which he gained of being a great divine.

At the age of twenty-six Mr. Shirreff received a call from the people in the parish of St. Ninians, Stirling, to become their minister. The heritors and people actually paid a very large sum of money to the patron to be allowed to have the man of their choice for their pastor. Strange as this reads to us, we suppose that it was by no means uncommon in those times, and at its worst was only a feeble imitation of the sales of livings, which are the shame and curse of the Church of England. Mr. Shirreff remained at St. Ninians, a faithful and beloved minister of the gospel for many years.

Mr. Haldane tells us that "Mr. Shirreff was, for many years, one of the most learned, popular, and impressive preachers in the Church of Scotland. He devoted himself much to study, and eagerly perused the writings of the Fathers, to which, besides those in his own valuable collection, he had access, through the Library which Archbishop Leighton had established at Dunblane, when he presided over that diocese. So much was Mr. Shirreff engaged in this study, that it was a common remark, when he was absent from the meetings of Presbytery, 'He is at home with his Fathers.' In the progress of his researches, he became satisfied that the attempted union of Church and State is Anti-Christian; and he was not disobedient to the heavenly oracle, 'Come out from among them, and be ye separate.' He resigned the charge of the parish of St. Ninians, in the Presbytery of Stirling, which he had held during thirty-five years," when he changed his views upon the subject of baptism and had to tear himself away, that he might maintain a conscience void of offence both towards God and towards man.

In 1823 he was baptized by the late Dr. Innes in Edinburgh, and received a call from the Baptist Church, meeting in Albion Street, Glasgow, to be their Pastor.

When he left St. Ninians, he had intended to reside in Edinburgh, but wishing to follow the leadings of Providence, he went to Glasgow, and laboured there for nine years. It was natural that he should wish to explain both to his old friends at St. Ninians, and to the community among which he had been a Presbyter, the reason for his change of views upon Baptism. *Hence the preparation and delivery of these Lectures,* which he delivered weekly on Wednesday evenings, in Albion Street Chapel, shortly after his settlement there. But though his courage and consistency required him to deliver these lectures, he did not feel bound to print them, and accordingly, as far as he was concerned, they would have passed away in the hearing, had not other voices prevailed after his decease. His full reliance upon the truth of believers' baptism made him feel that the New Testament was quite sufficient by itself to convince any intelligent Christian that believers should be immersed, and therefore he refused to publish his Lectures, or to prepare them for the press. It was a wise resolution which led to their being issued after his decease under the willing editorship of J. A. Haldane, Esq., who speaks of having corrected "trifling inaccuracies." We could have wished that Mr. Shirreff had been his own editor, for we have been compelled to grumble not a little at our esteemed predecessor for overlooking inaccuracies which were by no means trifling. Perhaps, however, some one else may follow *us* with the same criticism. An author can never be so well set forth as by himself. We have in a few passages found it difficult to guess at the Lecturer's meaning; and in the later lectures there are many omissions and abbreviations, which create obscurity and weaken force. How much we wish that Mr. Shirreff had superintended the press himself! Yet we have no difficulty whatever in sympathizing with his unwillingness to commit his lectures to the press. Often have we felt weary of the whole controversy, and utterly sick of the irrelevant matter dragged into it. It seems so clear. A New Testament appears to us to be the only argument needed, yet good people do not see what seems to us as clear as the sun at noonday. To be forced to argue year after year that ten and ten make twenty would not be more tiresome than to be forced to prove over and over again that which in the Scriptures of truth is written as with a sunbeam.

To return to Mr. Shirreff: in peace and happiness this good and great man laboured on in his new sphere till he entered into his rest in 1832, being then about seventy years of age; a shock of corn fully ripe.

So far we have sketched Mr. Shirreff's life; we cannot now do more than give remarks and incidents very much as we received them. It is too late in the day to attempt to make a biography or even an orderly record of leading facts.

Dr. Muir, of St. James', Glasgow, was accustomed to call Mr. Shirreff one of "the three mighties" in the Church of Scotland. Dr. Muir was at one time his assistant in the parish of St. Ninians. When preaching his trial sermon he said within himself "I am sure Mr. Shirreff and all the people are admiring me"—he had been studying elocution, and was displaying it. Mr. Shirreff waited for him when he came out of the pulpit, and taking his arm, said "Young man, if that is your style of preaching, you and I will not be long together; you have been preaching yourself, not Christ." To the honour of Dr. Muir let it be said, he did not resent this plain dealing, but profited by it, and became a thoroughly evangelical preacher. He often told the anecdote when in company, and said that Mr. Shirreff was the means of making him an efficient preacher.

In 1796 Mr. Charles Simeon attended a communion service in Stirling. On the Saturday he appears to have heard two preachers in succession, and by the time Mr. Shirreff had given a "further word of exhortation," four hours and a quarter had been spent in the services. Mr. Simeon seems to have thought that those who could profit by such lengthy services must have been made of different materials from himself, but he says of Mr. Shirreff's address, it was "short and affectionate, and seemed to arouse the congregation out of their lethargy; indeed, it was more to me than all the rest."

On the following Sabbath Mr. Simeon says, "Mr. Shirreff began the service, and preached a useful sermon from Hebrews x. 10. After preaching above an hour, besides prayer and singing, he left the pulpit and went to the head of the tables. There he gave an exhortation respecting the sacrament, which to me was more excellent than his sermon. He had some ideas that were new to me, viz., that on the day of atonement the high priest alone slew the sacrifices, intimating that Christ alone should perform the office of atoning. The other was, that before the offering of the incense, he had on the common garments of the priests, but afterwards his golden garments, intimating that Christ should be raised in a glorified body."

Mr. Shirreff appears to have asked Mr. Simeon to preach, but the elders made strong remarks in reference to "black prelacy," and it was not generally liked by the people. Mr. Simeon favours us in his letters with various criticisms upon Scotch worship, but he was probably unaware that he himself was being weighed in the balances by the sons of the Covenanters, with a result which would have startled his equanimity had it been communicated to him.

In 1804, Mr. Shirreff married Mary Russell,

daughter of Mr. Russell, minister in Stirling. She was one of the excellent of the earth, and greatly increased his usefulness. They often united in setting apart time for spreading out all their concerns before God. When any special matter called for it, days of fasting or thanksgiving were kept. Their minds, strengthened by communion with God, were strong for service or for suffering.

Mr. Shirreff was an early riser: from his diary it appears that he rose in summer at five o'clock, thus securing time for walking, and a certain number of hours each day for study, visiting, and prayer. When he went out before breakfast for his walk he was accustomed to go for some time, before he returned home, into a retired spot. As he remained there a long while every morning the curiosity of some who saw him was excited. A man followed him one morning and found that he, like Nathanael under the tree, made that his place for prayer. The man came away awe-struck.

In the evening he sometimes made one of the family circle, and read aloud a history, or some useful book. He took the trouble to teach his children Latin, Greek and French, and they soon found out that he was much more strict than their teacher at school. He conducted family worship three times a day—morning, noon and night. When his children were old enough, he took one of the questions of the Shorter Catechism at the end of each service, and instructed them in its meaning. They would gladly have dispensed with the exercise at the time, but in after life they found the instruction they had thus received invaluable:

their minds having been filled with good, sound scriptural doctrine, they were not carried away with the numberless errors of those with whom they came in contact in later years.

Mr. Shirreff aimed at excellence, not only in religion, but in everything else. We learn from his diary, in which he made an entry every day, how unreservedly he sought to bring all his powers of soul and body into complete subjection to the divine will. Though he had great gifts as a preacher, and was very highly esteemed and almost idolized by his people, yet during the first years of his ministry he had not that light and peace and joy which he afterwards realized. Often did he cry out with the apostle Paul, " O wretched man that I am ! who shall deliver me from the body of this death ? " Perhaps this experience was partly at least caused by the peculiar constitution of his mind, which would receive nothing without very clear and positive proof. He took occasion in after years to warn his family against the error into which he had fallen in this matter; for he had been tempted to question all the grand doctrines of the Gospel, and to examine the ground of the commonest truths of the Word. He studied hard in order to satisfy himself with regard to the evidences of Christianity, and the authenticity of the Scriptures, and as the result of his investigations he told his children, and also wrote in his diary, that he was thoroughly satisfied concerning the internal and external evidences of Christianity, and other questions about which his mind had been exercised, but that he had suffered much mental anxiety before he could arrive at that conclusion in consequence of his habit of requiring such convincing evidence of the point under consideration. Through the teaching of the Holy Spirit the issue to him was a full conviction of the truths which he held and taught, but he admitted that it was a dangerous path to follow,—a way in which the self-confidence of a man is more likely to be seen than the simple loving faith of a little child. Probably this explains how it was that in the earlier part of his ministry he did not receive the full assurance he desired, although he spent much time in prayer, and whole days in fasting and seeking direction from the Lord. This painful experience, however, was a grand preparation for his after work. The truths which he delivered were not his at second hand, but they had been wrought in him by the Spirit of God. By this process he also learned sympathy with the inward conflicts and mental doubts of those under his care. He preached as one who was intimately acquainted with the secret workings of his hearers' hearts, and in speaking to mourners in Zion he was peculiarly gentle and comforting. His own heart was very tender, and when speaking of divine things his feelings frequently overpowered him.

In reading the Scriptures the tones of his voice were most impressive. One person who heard him read the inspired account of the Lord's supper received therefrom her first right impressions of the nature and design of the ordinance. Once, when preaching about Caleb, the son of Jephunneh, his tone and manner in repeating the words of the Lord, "He had another spirit with him, and hath followed me fully," gave to one of his hearers a life-long impression of the wisdom of following God, whatever the multitude might do. He wrote out his sermons, but he never read them in the pulpit, and he did not like to hear other ministers read their discourses. He said that whatever labour it might involve he would really preach to the people. No doubt this helped to increase his popularity and usefulness. His library was well selected, and equally well used; the works of the old divines were his special favourites, and he made himself master of their contents. He was very fond of the writings of President Edwards, and often quoted one of his rules—" Resolved, to serve God, though no one else should do so."

Mr. Shirreff had a large Bible class in St. Ninians into which he admitted none younger than fifteen: many married people attended, while the assistant instructed the children. The larger catechism was the principal text-book, and much profit was derived from its study. The late Mr. Peter Drummond often spoke of the good received in this class, and formed one of a deputation from the class to present a testimonial to Mr. Shirreff after he had removed to Glasgow. As St. Ninians was a large parish, Mr. Shirreff had occasional meetings at different points within its bounds. On one occasion, visiting at a house where the servants were his hearers, although the master was an Episcopalian, he had a longing desire for the conversion of that gentleman, and prolonged his discourse hoping to reach his heart. At the close, Col.——, with great kindness, urged him to stay to dinner, though he seemed to be unaffected by the truth. Some time afterwards a young woman came to the manse, and applied to become a communicant at the Lord's Table. Mr. Shirreff was struck with her conversation, and asked when she had first begun to think about her soul. She said, "Do you remember, Sir, that day when you were at P——? I was in the dining-room of the house, and from that time I was awakened." After she had gone out Mr. Shirreff remarked to his wife, "How wonderful are the ways of God: I wished for the master, but he has given me the servant!"

At another time he was feeling unusually discouraged through not hearing of conversions amongst his people. He was riding out shortly afterwards to a distance to preach, and not knowing the road well he stopped to ask at a cottage. The person who opened the door said to him:— "I think, Sir, you are a clergyman; would you come in to see a dying man?" He went in, but he did not recognize the sick man, who seemed at once to know him and to brighten up. "Do you know me?" Mr. Shirreff asked. The man said, "I do not know your name, but I know your face; your sermon at Kippen, where I heard you preach, was the means of leading me to Christ." He deeply felt the goodness of God in permitting him, when desponding, to hear such good news of the blessing accompanying the word.

Mr. Shirreff kept a diary till the end of his life, but from 1796 it was written in short-hand, and with so many contractions of his own as to be illegible even to his sons, who were taught the same system that he used. It is therefore impossible to tell when he began to entertain doubts of the scripturalness of infant sprinkling. Afterwards when speaking of his altered views he affirmed that he set himself in earnest to ascertain the truth, and though he found it difficult in the midst of his manifold duties to devote so much time to the search, he took the trouble to examine all the classical writings which he had in his library, to find out the meaning of the word *baptizo*. Like Dr. Carson, he collated all the passages, and proved the meaning to be immersion. He most carefully examined the New Testament, and when he found that believers' baptism was of Divine appointment he at once resigned his charge. This, as we have before mentioned, was in 1823.

The Presbytery, unwilling to lose a minister so distinguished for piety and popular gifts, tried by every means to retain him, sending two ministers weekly to try to win him back. He had, however, counted the cost, and it was useless to seek to persuade him to withdraw his resignation. In the meantime, many infants were waiting to be baptized, and as the assistant minister, not being ordained, could not baptize them, and Mr. Shirreff would not, the poor little dears were left for awhile as Christ intended them to remain until they grew up, and believed on him. Mrs. Shirreff, who did not then fully understand her husband's change of views, said that there was a great talk in the country about his refusing to baptize the infants, and she thought as the Presbytery would not accept his resignation that he should in the meantime baptize the children. His reply was a right noble one, "How can I stand up to baptize an infant *in the name*, which means amongst other things, by the authority of God the Father, God the Son, and God the Holy Ghost, although there is no such authority, and *I know there is no such authority?* I would not do it for the world."

She never asked him again, but was herself afterwards baptized according to the scriptural fashion.

Some of the ministers were very angry with Mr. Shirreff for resigning his charge, especially one or two of the "moderate" clergy, who would have "censured" him, but the other members of the Presbytery would not suffer it, but accepted his resignation.

It was a painful season when he parted from his beloved people, many of whom were bound to him by spiritual ties; giving up his large income, leaving the manse which had been built for him, and meeting with reproach; but "he endured, as seeing him who is invisible." He preached his farewell sermon from Acts xx. 32: "And now, brethren, I commend you to God, and to the word of his grace, which is able to build you up, and to give you an inheritance among all them which are sanctified." The large old church, always full when he preached, was crowded. The sight of the preacher's face was touching, as he stood up with hands uplifted in prayer: his quivering lips and faltering voice showed that he was scarcely able to control his emotion, but God graciously strengthened his servant, and enabled him to preach in his usual faithful and impressive manner.

The people waited for him, and lined all the road to the Manse. He was unable to speak, but covered his eyes with one hand, and held out the other to his dear people.

He went to Edinburgh in the beginning of the same week, and was there baptized by the late Dr. Innes.

As we have already intimated, he had purposed retiring to Edinburgh, but the Baptist Church, meeting in Albion Street, Glasgow, sent him an invitation, which he accepted. On one occasion one of his people from St. Ninians hearing him preach on "Obey them that have the rule over you, and submit yourselves," came into the vestry after service and said, "Oh, Sir, I hope they are not using you ill here." He assured her that the people in Glasgow were kind to him. A singular incident occurred in connection with his leaving St. Ninians. The godly people there had formed prayer meetings, the men meeting with Mr. Shirreff, the females with Mrs. Shirreff. The members of these prayer meetings were sorely grieved about their pastor leaving, and spoke in such a way as to grieve Mrs. Shirreff. She told them that "it was not to fill a Professor's chair that he was leaving them, but for conscience' sake." One of the members of Mr. Shirreff's meeting was loud in his complaints, and the utterances of such a godly man increased the bitterness of the trial of the conscientious minister.

This old gentleman had a son in Glasgow, a doctor in good practice, and, after Mr. Shirreff settled in Glasgow, this gentleman, who was a Unitarian, sent to say that he wished to see his father's late clergyman. Mr. Shirreff called on him, and found him ill in bed. He explained that he had sent for Mr. Shirreff to repay a small sum of money he borrowed from him at college. Mr.

Shirreff had no recollection of it till he told him, but said " We will now speak of more important things," and began gently to open a conversation about spiritual matters. The sick man kindly invited him to return the next day, and each day begged to have another interview. At last he told his servants to tell his own minister (a Unitarian) when he called that he could not see him, as Mr. Shirreff was visiting him. One day Mr. Shirreff said to his wife, with tears in his eyes, " This is a remarkable case, Dr. B. is receiving the gospel." The gratitude and love of the dying man were very great to the instrument which the Lord had used to his salvation. He died, and on the day of the funeral the aged father came up from St. Ninians, and it was touching to see the aged man, with snow-white hair and tear-filled eyes, go up to Mr. Shirreff, before all the people, and beg his forgiveness for the unkind words he had spoken to him when he was leaving St. Ninians. He said, " Oh sir, I was wrong ; if you had not come to Glasgow, my son would have gone to hell."

The late Dr. James Hamilton, of London, when a student in Glasgow, took seats in Albion Street Chapel. He wrote after Mr. Shirreff's death to Mrs. Shirreff, "that it had never been his lot to hear such masterly expositions of Scripture as then."

Mr. Shirreff continued in Glasgow to set apart time for seeking counsel of God : he often said he was saved from much trouble and loss by doing so. On the last day of the year he was accustomed to remain for some hours alone, and after breakfast all the members of the family were called in. He first read a portion of Scripture containing a confession of sin, with a corresponding psalm, and offered an appropriate prayer, then another portion, thanking God for the mercies of the past year, and closed with a prayer for all needed blessings and direction for the ensuing year.

His prayers on ordinary days at family worship, held twice a day in Glasgow, were usually taken from the chapter read, which he turned into prayer.

He had a great reverence for God. Sometimes in prayer, like Abraham, he threw himself prostrate on the ground before the Most High God.

One Sabbath day, between the services, one of his sons went suddenly into the library, without knocking as usual at the door. He found his dear father in prayer in that attitude, prostrated before God, and the boy came out with tears in his eyes.

It is no wonder that such a parent's holy example and constant self-denial impressed his family.

Though so devout he was not gloomy, but cheerful and witty in company. In his diary he constantly complains of his own want of gravity.

During the visitation of cholera in Glasgow, Mr. Shirreff asked his people to set apart a day for fasting and prayer that the Lord would preserve them from its attacks. Sceptics may question the value of prayer, but the fact remains that not one member of the Church or congregation was attacked by the terrible disease. Verily God does hear the cry of his children.

When Mr. Shirreff's health began to fail he was urged by his son, a medical student, to retire to the country, but he would not be persuaded, and continued to preach till within five weeks of his death. At the time that his last illness commenced the Church met and fasted, and prayed for his recovery, but it was not the will of God to grant their request. His servant's labours were ended, and he was going home.

When one of his children went into his room during the last week of his life, he said to her, "M——., take care that you are found on the side of truth; take care that you are not ashamed of the truth." She burst into tears as the thought forced itself upon her mind that her dear father believed himself to be dying.

The doctor who was attending him proposed a consultation, as he was suffering from chronic catarrh, and a complication of complaints. When the doctors were with him, one of them said to him, "You will soon be in a better world, sir." He did not answer, but as soon as they were gone he lifted up his eyes and hands to heaven, saying, "O God, I thank thee that this does not give me a painful surprise." At another time he said, "The gospel is our only resource when we come here."

He also took the hand of his dear wife in his, saying, "You have nobly discharged relative duties to me."

On the day before his death his face shone with a supernatural brightness, and he said to Mrs. Shirreff, "Who are these? What fine singing!" She told him that there was no one there, but he pointed to the top of the bed and exclaimed, "They are there. What fine singing!" He spoke constantly till he died, but his speech was inarticulate.

The following morning at nine o'clock he entered into rest, having nearly reached the allotted threescore years and ten.

A man who so lived, and so died, deserves to be heard when speaking upon the subject out of which grew the trial of his life. He being dead yet speaketh : God grant that his voice may be heard.

C. H. S.

LECTURES ON BAPTISM.

INTRODUCTORY LECTURE.

IMPORTANCE OF POSITIVE INSTITUTIONS, AND OBSERVATIONS ON THE ORDINANCE OF BAPTISM.

THE object of these Lectures is to state the doctrine of the Scriptures on the ordinance of Christian Baptism. It is a very common, though a very groundless and hurtful opinion, that the discussion of this subject is unnecessary. Positive institutions are far from being uninteresting to the friends of religion; in them the truth is embodied, and the observance of them, as of every precept of revelation, belongs to the obedience of faith, and comfort of the gospel. We have salutary warning in the Scriptures, that it is at our peril if we act on the popular error that positive institutions are unworthy of study and attention. "He that despised Moses' law, died without mercy under two or three witnesses: of how much sorer punishment, suppose ye, shall he be thought worthy, who hath .... done despite unto the Spirit of grace?" Heb. x. 29. "The Lord smote the men of Beth-shemesh, because they had looked into the ark of the Lord, even he smote of the people fifty thousand and threescore and ten men": 1 Sam. vi. 19. "And when they came to Nachon's threshing-floor, Uzzah put forth his hand to the ark of God, and took hold of it; for the oxen shook it. And the anger of the Lord was kindled against Uzzah; and God smote him there for his error; and there he died by the ark of God": 2 Sam. vi. 6, 7. "Wherefore, whosoever shall eat this bread, and drink this cup of the Lord unworthily, shall be guilty of the body and blood of the Lord. But let a man examine himself, and so let him eat of that bread, and drink of that cup. For he that eateth and drinketh unworthily, eateth and drinketh judgment to himself, not discerning the Lord's body. For this cause many are weak and sickly among you, and many sleep. For if we would judge ourselves, we should not be judged": 1 Cor. xi. 27—31.

James, speaking of violating a positive injunction, viz. having respect of persons in church associations, represents it as a violation of the whole law. "But if ye have respect to persons, ye commit sin, and are convinced of the law as transgressors. For whosoever shall keep the whole law, and yet offend in one point, he is guilty of all": James ii. 9, 10. And speaking of the commandments, whether positive or moral, our Lord says, "Whosoever therefore shall break one of these least commandments, and shall teach men so, he shall be called the least in the kingdom of heaven: but whosoever shall do and teach them, the same shall be called great in the kingdom of heaven": Matt. v. 19.

Our consciences are charged with the study of the doctrine of baptism, by peculiar and affecting considerations. It occupies a large proportion of New Testament revelation. From the line of positive institutions, baptism stands prominently out, and attracts special attention. "Go ye into all the world, and preach the gospel to every creature He that believeth and is baptized shall be saved": Mark xvi. 15—16. "Jesus answered, Verily, verily, I say unto thee, except a man be born of water and of the Spirit, he cannot enter into the kingdom of God": John iii. 5. "The like figure whereunto baptism doth also now save us, (not the putting away the filth of the flesh, but the answer of a good conscience toward God,) by the resurrection of Jesus Christ": 1 Peter iii. 21. The interests of the Church of Christ are deeply concerned in the scriptural administration, and, of course, in the diligent study of this ordinance. Baptism, like every other ordinance, must be administered in the name of God. Suppose, for a moment, that the administrator proceeds in this name, whilst he cannot produce his mandate, he proceeds in profanation of the dreadful name of Jehovah. Whoever countenances or encourages the profanation, makes the guilt his own, and subjects himself to the consequences. Suppose a parent to misunderstand this ordinance; he not only himself sins against God, but throws in the way of his child obstructions which he may never be able to surmount. Suppose a missionary to introduce amongst the heathen a corrupt administration of this ordinance; ages may be required to remove the corruption.

The Churches of Christ are at present most unhappily divided, and until this institution be honestly studied, and rightly observed, these mortifying divisions can never be healed.

The study of the subject is pressed on the conscience of each individual, by a regard to his own interest. The Christian world is divided; the question is practical; I must bear witness in one way or another. If I have not studied the subject, how do I know that I am not bearing false witness against my neighbour; calling good evil, and evil good; instead of making my light so shine before men, that others may see my good works, and glorify God? If I have not studied the subject, how do I know that I am not, by my example, misleading others, and bringing myself under the woe denounced in Matthew xviii. 7: "Woe unto the world because of offences! for it must needs be that offences come; but woe to that man by whom the offence cometh!" "Whatsoever is not of faith is sin": Rom. xiv. 23. "Faith cometh by hearing, and hearing by the word of God": Rom. x. 17. Consequently, if I cannot from the word of God vindicate my practice to my own mind, I sin against God. It ought never to be forgotten, that ignorance is no valid plea. "That servant which knew his lord's will, and prepared not himself, neither did according to his will, shall be beaten with many stripes. But he that knew not, and did commit things worthy of stripes, shall be beaten with few stripes": Luke xii. 47.

Hence, the reiterated command to search the Scriptures, John v. 39; to prove all things, and to hold fast that which is good: 1 Thess. v. 21.

Those who fear God, who respect the interest of the Church, of the public, of themselves, or of their relatives, must have anticipated the conclusion, that Baptism should be diligently studied.

The faithful disciple of Christ must, in Baptism, as in every other branch of ecclesiastical polity, examine, judge, and act for himself. The great mass of our race are the slaves of human authority. In heathen countries, the population is generally heathen ; Mahommedan, under the government of the Turk. In some countries, infants are immersed; in this country they are generally sprinkled. Thus, according to the fashion, men are Papists, or Protestants, Episcopalians, Presbyterians, or Independents. The great majority of men are the creatures of external condition, of fashion, of interest, and similar influences.

The Christian has renounced the world ; and here, as in other things, he must justify his profession. The law is, "Call no man your father upon the earth ; for one is your Father, which is in heaven": Matt. xxiii. 9. "If ye be dead with Christ from the rudiments of the world, why, as though living in the world, are ye subject to ordinances . . . . after the commandments and doctrines of men?" Col. ii. 20. In Rev. ii. and iii. how often is it repeated, "He that hath an ear, let him hear what the Spirit saith to the churches."

The design of these Lectures will not be altogether frustrated, if, by their means, any shall be induced to lay aside prejudice, to examine for themselves, and for themselves to decide and act in regard to this important ordinance of Christ.

The object of these Discourses is to assist the

honest inquirer in his search after truth. When he is in danger of being misled by habit, misrepresentation, or sophistry, he must be apprised of his danger; these habits, misrepresentations, and sophistries must be exposed. Beyond this necessary duty, every thing polemical and controversial will be avoided. It is with doctrines that the enquirer after truth is concerned. The grand question is—"What saith the Scripture?" Having ascertained this, it ought to be of no moment by whom the doctrine is either taught or received, opposed or rejected.

It is the desire and duty of the speaker to assist the honest and enlightened part of the community in detecting and removing the corruptions of Christianity. This design would be frustrated by the perversion, misrepresentation, or misapplication of any part of Scripture. Inquirers therefore may depend on it, that, according to the grace given, the example of the Apostle will be followed: " Seeing we have this ministry, as we have received mercy, we faint not; but have renounced the hidden things of dishonesty, not walking in craftiness, nor handling the word of God deceitfully; but by manifestation of the truth commending ourselves to every man's conscience in the sight of God ": 2 Cor. iv. 1.

In order to profit by these Lectures, the following hints may be useful :—

1. *Continue in prayer to God for the direction and guidance of the Spirit.* "What man is he that feareth the Lord? Him shall he teach in the way that he shall choose": Ps. xxv. 12. "If ye, then, being evil, know how to give good gifts to your

children: how much more shall your heavenly Father give the Holy Spirit to them that ask Him?" Luke xi. 13.

2. *Whilst any particular topic is under discussion, we should confine our attention to that particular topic.* Of that exclusively it will be our interest to think and determine. For instance, the inquiry whether Christians, after believing, ought to be baptized, does not involve the consideration of infant baptism. Again, supposing infant baptism to be commanded, the question whether this should supersede our observance of Baptism after believing, is distinct from both the preceding inquiries.

3. *The inquirer should be on his guard against the effects of remaining corruption and external influence.* Many good men (like the first Reformers) have never studied these subjects. Some of approved character and learning have defended corruptions of the truth by arguments which prove only the power of preconceived opinions. In the ordinary affairs of life, the man would be pitied who had the weakness seriously to advance such arguments. The influence of corruption remaining in the mind is still more to be dreaded. He has little to expect from the assistance of others, who is not continually on his guard against it.

4. *The inquirer must himself read through the New Testament;* he must observe all the passages which treat on the subject of Baptism at one, or rather at different readings; he must observe what each passage intimates on the different topics of inquiry. Having finished this process, he must mark the result. If he reads other books (as he probably will), he must act in regard to his books,

as a judge or a jury acts in regard to counsel: having heard both sides, they decide for themselves. I said, books besides the New Testament will probably be read; but allow me to say also, that this labour is not absolutely necessary. The Scriptures themselves are sufficient to make the man of God perfect, thoroughly furnished to every good work. But whether other books be perused or not, the inquirer must begin and end with the perusal of the New Testament. The Spirit of God must have the honour which is exclusively due to himself. The inquirer will find that submission to God, and the enjoyment of him, are here, as everywhere else, inseparably connected.

Of the reasonings of men we shall treat in their place; at present, I give only the following cautions:—Never mistake suppositions or mere assertions for proofs. Never act on a proof proposed, but not understood. Never confound the creatures of imagination with the conclusions of reason. Never mistake one subject for another, but distinguish things that differ.

LECTURE II.

NATURE OF THE EVIDENCE REQUIRED.

THE object of this Lecture is to ascertain the kind of evidence required in discussions on Baptism. Inattention to this has occasioned much unproductive labour. The candid inquirer will consult both his duty and comfort, by recollecting the truth and consequences of the following positions.

POSITION I. The Scriptures of truth are the only rule to direct us how, in this ordinance, as in every thing else, God is to be glorified and enjoyed.

These words are used partly because they express what is intended, and partly because they anticipate the objection from novelty. Minute attention to what God appoints is repeatedly enjoined both in the Old and in the New Testaments. "Now therefore hearken, O Israel, unto the statutes and unto the judgments which I teach you, for to do them. Ye shall not add unto the word which I command you, neither shall ye diminish ought from it, that ye may keep the commandments of the Lord your God which I command you". Deut. iv. 1, 2. "And the Lord said unto me, Son of man, mark well, and behold with thine eyes, and hear with thine ears all that I say unto thee concerning all the ordinances of the house of the Lord, and all the laws thereof; and mark well the entering in of the house, with every going forth of the sanctuary": Ezekiel xliv. 5. "To the law and to the testimony: if they speak not according to this word, it is because there is no light in them": Isaiah viii. 20. "Now we command you, brethren, in the name of our Lord Jesus Christ, that ye withdraw yourselves from every brother that walketh disorderly, and not after the tradition which he received of us": 2 Thess. iii. 6. "Hold fast the form of sound words, which thou hast heard of me, in faith and love which is in Christ Jesus": 2 Tim. i. 13. "All Scripture is given by inspiration of God, and is profitable for doctrine, for reproof, for correction, for instruction in righteousness: that the man of God may be perfect, throughly furnished unto all good works": 2 Tim. iii. 16, 17. "We are of God: he that knoweth God heareth us: he that is not of God heareth not us. Hereby know we the spirit of truth, and the spirit of error": 1 John iv. 6. But I need not multiply proofs. The truth of the doctrine is incontestable. Let us mark the consequence. Arguments for the baptism or sprinkling of infants, if drawn from any other source than the Scriptures, cannot bind the conscience. Of this description are arguments taken from the practice of Pædo-baptists, ancient or modern—arguments founded on the piety, learning, and numbers of such as baptize, or sprinkle infants—arguments founded on the writings of the Jewish Rabbins, and the alleged practice of the Jews in admitting their proselytes—arguments founded on the writings of the Fathers and Church historians—arguments founded on the authority of assemblies and councils—arguments founded on the supposed congruity and utility of baptizing or sprinkling infants. The inquirer, on reflection, must refer to the same class all arguments which he finds he does not understand.

All the evidence in these circumstances resolves itself into a regard to human authority. To all these and similar arguments the candid inquirer will reply: The Scriptures alone must determine my faith; if I find that in the Scriptures I am directed to baptize or sprinkle my infants, they must be baptized or sprinkled accordingly, whatever the contrary practice may have been, how long soever it may have existed, and how extensively soever it may have prevailed; whatever be the piety, learning, or numbers of its opponents: whatever be the doctrine of Jewish Rabbins or Christian Fathers; whatever be the pretences of congruity or utility; or whatever opinion I may entertain of the learning of the advocates of the opposite practice.

On the contrary, if I find no instructions in the Scriptures either to baptize or sprinkle infants, I can neither immerse nor sprinkle them (be the practices and opinions of men what they may) without violating my allegiance to the God of the Scriptures, and contracting the guilt of will-worship.

I repeat the conclusion: if a man have ability and inclination to study the writings of the Jews, the Fathers, and Church historians: if he wishes to know the history of Baptism, and of Councils, he may indulge his curiosity; but his conscience must be directed by the Bible alone.

Position II. The Scriptures *of the New Testament* are the only rule to direct us as to the positive institutions of the Gospel Dispensation.

First, we must prove the truth of the position, and then mark its bearings on the subject before us.

Before, however, we adduce the proof, allow me, in order to secure attention to it, to premise one of the designs of proving a position so obviously true.

From our earliest years, we have been accustomed to associate the ideas of the Lord's-supper and the passover, of circumcision and baptism, of Abraham and his posterity with parents and their children; with what propriety or impropriety we shall afterwards inquire. It is a fact, that such an association of ideas generally exists. In some of us, it has grown with our growth, and strengthened with our strength. Certain teachers have not failed to avail themselves of the prejudice. By it, they have led us to visionary speculations respecting the covenants with Noah, Abraham, and Moses. Their object is frequently gained. Men who are not indisposed to be misled, easily find an excuse for gratifying their wishes. Honest inquirers, perplexed and confused by the general practice, and distrustful of their own judgments, hesitate to practise what they know, and perhaps altogether abandon their inquiries after truth.

To the first of these classes I have at present nothing to say. To the second, all attention is due. Their duty is plain. Having learned from the New Testament the mind of the Lord, let them act on their convictions, though they may feel the influence of early prejudices, and though there be still many things in the Old Dispensation which they are not able fully to explain.

I proceed to prove, that if any, through prejudice, should imagine that the doctrines of the New Testament are inconsistent with the institutions of the Old, then the obscure passages in the Old Testament must be explained by the clear passages in the New. I am not to darken my views of the New Testament by looking at it only through the vail of the Old.

I. Observe, first, that *the Old Dispensation is come to an end, and all its positive institutions, that is to say, its ceremonial observances, are abrogated.* Before we produce the proof of this assertion, the doctrine must be distinctly stated. It will be of considerable advantage to the inquirer fully to understand it. Mistake or misrepresentation here has given a degree of plausibility to arguments, the fallacy of which would otherwise have been obvious. First, then, let it be noticed, that the plan of redemption, or the covenant of grace, as it is commonly called, is always the same. It admits of no change. It is the same under the New Dispensation that it was under the Old. Men have always been saved in the same way, whether under the Christian economy, or under the Mosaic, Abrahamic, or more ancient branches of the Old Dispensation.

Let it also be noticed that there are two distinct dispensations, and but two. The Old Testament, and the New Testament; or, as they are generally denominated, the Law and the Gospel. The Old

Dispensation had four branches; the first, reaching from Adam to Noah; the second, from Noah to Abraham; the third, from Abraham to Moses; the fourth, from Moses to Christ. These four branches are distinct, but the dispensation is one, namely, the Law, or Old Testament. Let it be noticed, thirdly, that the positive institutions flowed down, and increased, until they all met, and were absorbed in the Mosaical branch of that dispensation. Thus from Adam to Noah we find sacrifices, but no other positive institutions. Sacrifices are carried forward into the branch under Noah; the prohibition of blood is added, perhaps the payment of tithes, and the distinction of animals into *clean* and *unclean*.

These are carried forward into the branch from Abraham, and circumcision is added. All these together are carried forward into the branch from Moses to Christ. The ceremonial was then completed, and remained in force until it was fulfilled and abolished by Christ. Thus the Saviour, speaking of circumcision, says, "Moses therefore gave unto you circumcision; (not because it is of Moses, but of the fathers;) and ye on the sabbath day circumcise a man. If a man on the sabbath day receive circumcision, that the law of Moses should not be broken; are ye angry at me, because I have made a man every whit whole on the sabbath day?" John vii. 22, 23. Observe, that it was given by Moses, and belonged to his law; but that it was not originally of Moses, being introduced into his law from the branch of the dispensation under the patriarchs. Let it be noticed farther, that the characters of the Old and New Dispensations of the covenant of grace are different. The Old is prophecy; the New is fulfilment. "All the prophets and the law prophesied until John": Matt. xi. 13. Christ came to fulfil these prophecies. "Think not that I am come to destroy the law, or the prophets: I am not come to destroy, but to fulfil": Matt. v. 17. The Old Dispensation is the painting, the shadow, the type. The New is the original, the substance, the antitype. "The law was given by Moses; but grace and truth came by Jesus Christ": John i. 17. Truth is opposed not only to falsehood, but to type and shadow. (See Daniel vii. 19; John iv. 24). The Old Dispensation is promise; the New is performance. "For all the promises of God in him are yea, and in him Amen, unto the glory of God by us": 2 Cor. i. 20. The contrast is noted in many other ways in the Scriptures: the *letter* and the *spirit;* the *servant* and the *son*, and the like. Hence, the type and the antitype are often described in the same words. "David" is used to signify both the son of Jesse, and David's son and Lord. God is the God of Abraham, and of his seed, both in a typical and antitypical sense. The apostle reasons from the type to the antitype. "Abraham had two sons," &c., Gal. iv. 22—31.

Carrying these things along with us, we proceed to prove the assertion that the Old Dispensation, in all its branches, is at an end, and all its positive institutions abrogated. This the judaizing teachers denied; they taught that men must be circumcised, and keep the law of Moses. Many in our own time teach things of the same kind. As to the doctrine of Baptism, they say, that, excepting the mode of administration, baptism is circumcision, and circumcision baptism; and that unless a law of repeal be produced, we must baptize according to the law of circumcision. The law of repeal I am now to produce.

The Lord by Jeremiah, ch. xxxi. 31—34, promises to make a new covenant with the house of Israel, and with the house of Judah, and the apostle, after quoting the passage, says,—" In that he saith, A new covenant, he hath made the first old. Now that which decayeth and waxeth old, is ready to vanish away": Heb. viii. 13. Surely that which has vanished away is repealed, and the repeal of the covenant implies the repeal of all its ordinances. Again the apostle, after quoting Hag. ii. 6, says, "Whose voice then shook the earth: but now he hath promised, saying, Yet once more I shake not the earth only, but also heaven. And this word, Yet once more, signifieth the removing of those things that are shaken, as of things that are made, that those things which cannot be shaken may remain": Heb. xii. 26, 27. Here we are expressly taught that the things that were shaken were *removed*, evidently referring to the positive observances of the Old Dispensation, among which *circumcision* was one, John vii. 23; while the great principle of love, which is the end of the law, must for ever remain. The Apostle then proceeds to glory in the stability of the New Dispensation: "Wherefore we, receiving a kingdom which *cannot be moved*, let us have grace," &c. Again, he says, "If that which was *done away* was glorious, much more that which *remaineth* is glorious," and represents Israel as unable to look to the end of that which is *abolished:* 2 Cor. iii. 11—13. In these, and many other passages, we are explicitly taught that the Old Dispensation, with all its rites and ordinances, is at an end, and consequently, it is unlawful for us to observe any of the positive institutions of this abrogated dispensation.

Accordingly, a great part of the New Testament is employed, in opposition to the judaizing teachers, in asserting *the liberty of Christians from the laws of the Old Dispensation.* The writing of the Old Dispensation is called the Old Testament, the law and the prophets, and particularly "Moses"; because the Mosaic branch of the Old Dispensation included the three preceding branches. This writing begins with Genesis, and ends with Malachi, and comprehends all the branches of the first dispensation. "But their minds were blinded: for until this day remaineth the same vail untaken away in the reading of the Old Testament; which vail is done away in Christ. But even unto this day, when Moses is read, the vail is upon their heart": 2 Cor. iii. 14, 15.

Notwithstanding all this, it is urged that we are still more or less bound by the law of circumcision: " though the form be altered," it is said, " the substance, the spirit of circumcision, the thing itself, is binding; at least so far as the subjects of baptism are concerned." But, it is answered, the whole consists of all the parts; and if the whole be abolished, every part must be abolished. This pertinacity, however, obliges me to refer to one example of the many scriptures which declare that circumcision, in particular, is abrogated. "Behold, I Paul say unto you, that if ye be circumcised,

Christ shall profit you nothing. For I testify *again* to every man that is circumcised, that he is a debtor to do the whole law. Christ is become of no effect unto you": Gal. v. 3. Here the apostle expressly declares, that the law of circumcision is abrogated. Circumcision is abolished; not the name merely, nor some special ritual connected therewith, but circumcision itself is abolished. It is not sprinkling with water, instead of the effusion of blood, not the form of administration that is altered, but *circumcision itself is abolished.**

---

* The reader is referred to Acts xv. 24—29; Gal. iv. 9; v. 2—6; vi. 12—15; Philip. iii. 3; Col. ii. 11.

LECTURE III.

THE NEW TESTAMENT THE ONLY RULE IN REGARD TO THE POSITIVE INSTITUTIONS OF THE GOSPEL.

THE position under consideration is, That *the Scriptures of the New Testament are the only rule to direct us in regard to the positive institutions of the Gospel*; and of this position the first proof is, that the Old Dispensation is at an end.

From the Old Dispensation, arguments have been drawn in support of the pontificate, the gradations of the hierarchy, the establishment and materials of national churches, the payment of tithes, and, what is before us, the baptism or sprinkling of infants. But the Old Dispensation is at an end. *Are we, then, to baptize or sprinkle our infants, because infants under the law were circumcised?* In the business of life, the plea would be treated with scorn. Suppose an advocate, in pleading for his client, should seriously urge the customs and laws of a foreign country, or an act of parliament that had long ago been repealed; what judge or jury would endure such impertinence? Should a person raise an action for recovering a debt, on a deed bearing legal evidence that the debt had been paid, and the deed cancelled; what advocate would undertake the cause, or what court would for a moment listen to the pleader? Yet this is the very pith and strength of the argument for baptizing or sprinkling infants. The whole rests on institutions that have been abrogated for nearly eighteen hundred years, or rather on inferences from these institutions. What at present we plead for, is, that the doctrine of Baptism must be learned, not from the institutions of the Old Economy, but from the Scriptures of the New Testament. As to inferences, their weight in the present question shall afterwards be considered. In the meantime, allow me to observe, that an inference from nothing amounts to nothing. Should I, without foundation, infer that I shall have an estate; what would a sober man think of my state of mind, or of my prospects?

Hitherto, we have said that Pædo-baptism or sprinkling can neither be founded on the law of circumcision, nor inferred from it. The reason has been produced; the Old Economy, in general, and circumcision, in particular, are abrogated. This fact, however, namely, the termination of the Old Economy, will carry us farther. Though infants had been not only circumcised, but baptized, under the abrogated dispensation, they could not, *without a new law*, be baptized under the Gospel Dispensation. A merchant gives a commission to his agent; if he withdraw that commission, his agent cannot act on the commission now withdrawn: farther agency, though by the same person, and in the same department, requires a new commission. The application is obvious; we are not subject to the law of an abrogated dispensation. I repeat, that we have but to transfer to the ordinary business of life the arguments for infant baptism, and their futility will instantly appear.

Thus it appears that the old dispensation of the

Covenant of Grace, in all its branches, is at an end. The existing dispensation is the Gospel; and it is from the record of that dispensation, the New Testament, that we must take our instructions respecting its positive institutions.

Besides, there is nothing taught in the Old Testament respecting baptism; the obvious consequence is, the truth of the position under consideration, that the Scriptures of the New Testament are the only rule to direct us as to this and other positive institutions of the Gospel dispensation.

II. *The sacred writers call the Gospel dispensation a New Dispensation;* Pædo-baptists take the opposite side: they would carry us back to the weak and beggarly elements of Judaism; some have argued in favour of national covenanting connected with the identity of the Old and New Testament Churches; all in one way or another deny that the Gospel dispensation is *new*. The doctrine, therefore, must be proved.

We need not again be reminded that the covenant of grace is under every dispensation the same. We are to prove that the dispensation is *new*, and confine ourselves, to avoid unnecessary discussions, to its positive institutions. "For, behold, I create new heavens and a new earth: and the former shall not be remembered nor come into mind": Isaiah lxv. 17. "Behold, the days come, saith the Lord, that I will make a new covenant with the house of Israel, and with the house of Judah": Jeremiah xxxi. 31. "Old things are passed away; behold, all things are become new": 2 Cor. v. 17.

The preaching of John the Baptist and the Apostles is called "the beginning of the Gospel", Mark i. 1, &c.; again we read, in 1 Cor. xi. 25, "After the same manner also he took the cup, when he had supped, saying, This cup is the *New* Testament in my blood". Hence the writings of this dispensation are commonly and rightly termed the New Testament. What, then, is the duty of the inquirer? There are two Testaments before him; the one declared by God to be *old* and *vanished away*: the other *new* and *everlasting*. By which ought he to regulate his practice? The very existence of the Testament, entitled New by the Lord of our consciences, determines the matter. A master calls his servant from one work, and appoints him to perform another; a dutiful servant will act by the instructions last received. We are urged to carry the former state of things along with us. The Scriptures quoted teach us a very different doctrine. The era with which Mark begins his history is the beginning of the Gospel. It is there, and *not before*, that we are to begin to learn the institutions of the Gospel. Without knowing, then, the contents of the Old Testament, or of the New, the titles Old and New suggest, as soon as observed, expectations directly the reverse of what is suggested in the arguments for sprinkling of infants.* I expect to

---

* All must admit that baptism is an ordinance of the new covenant, and surely nothing can be more evident than that the ordinances of the new covenant are intended only for the children of that covenant. Now, all the children of the new covenant, from the least to the greatest, know the Lord, and to such, so far as we can ascertain, is the ordinance of baptism to be confined.—H.

find changes in the dispensation, numerous and great; and what these changes are can be learned only from the New Testament. One word more, and I conclude this proof of our second position. If I find, as the inquirer certainly will, that in the New Testament the whole doctrine of Baptism is cleary revealed, I must act on this paramount evidence, although I feel the influence of inveterate, but groundless associations. This feeling will gradually subside, light will gradually increase, every day I shall be more and more led to esteem all the precepts of my Lord concerning all things to be right, and to hate every false way. "If any man will do His will, he shall know of the doctrine, whether it be of God".

III. *Christ exclusively is Lord of the New Dispensation.* "God hath made him both Lord and Christ": Acts ii. 36. "All power is given unto me in heaven and in earth": Matt. xxviii. 18. "The Son of man is Lord also of the Sabbath": Mark ii. 28. In this relation, Christ is preferred to Moses. "The Lord thy God will raise up unto thee a Prophet from the midst of thee, of thy brethren, like unto me; unto Him ye shall hearken". "I will raise them up a Prophet from among their brethren, like unto thee (Moses), and will put my words in his mouth; and he shall speak unto them all that I shall command him. And it shall come to pass, that whosoever will not hearken unto my words which he shall speak in my name, I will require it of him": Deut. xviii. 15, 18. While Peter spake to the Lord on the Mount of transfiguration, "Behold a bright cloud overshadowed them; and behold a voice out of the cloud, which said, This is my beloved Son, in whom I am well pleased; *hear ye him*": Matt. xvii. 5. It will be recollected, that when this voice was heard, Moses and Elias were with Christ on the mount. There cannot be a doubt that the vision is recorded to call the attention of men from the servant to the Son, from Moses to Christ. "For unto the angels hath he not put in subjection the world to come (the Gospel Dispensation), of which we speak". "And Moses, verily, was faithful in all his house, as a servant, for a testimony of those things which were to be spoken after; but Christ as a Son over his own house." "Wherefore, holy brethren, partakers of the heavenly calling, consider the Apostle and High Priest of *our* profession, *Christ Jesus*". Heb. ii. 5; iii. 5, 6; iii. 1. The "Lord" is the ordinary title which the disciples give to their Master; and that we may not mistake their meaning, they frequently tell us, and in a great variety of language, that "he is Lord of all": Acts x. 36.

From whom, then, are we to receive our instructions respecting the positive institutions of the Gospel Dispensation? The answer is plain; we must receive all our instructions from the Lord and Apostle of our profession, Christ Jesus. It is not to the purpose to say, that the whole Scriptures are dictated by the Spirit of Christ. Our duty is plain from Hebrews i. 1: "God, who at sundry times and in divers manners, spake in time past unto the fathers by the prophets, hath in these last days spoken unto us by His Son." Him, therefore, we must hear.

IV. *The Apostles were exclusively commissioned to make known to the churches the commands of their King.* Them he chose, them he qualified, them he commissioned to execute this trust. It was into their hands exclusively that he committed the keys of his kingdom. "I will give unto thee (Peter and the other Apostles) the keys of the kingdom of heaven: and whatsoever thou shalt bind on earth shall be bound in heaven: and whatsoever thou shalt loose on earth shall be loosed in heaven": Matt. xvi. 19. "And Jesus said unto them (the Apostles), Verily, I say unto you, that when the Son of man shall sit in the throne of his glory (the ascension of Christ), ye also shall sit upon twelve thrones, judging the twelve tribes of Israel"; (Matt. xix. 28;) that is, Ye shall have the honour of publishing the laws, and introducing the ordinances of the dispensation of the Gospel. "He that heareth you heareth me: and he that despiseth you despiseth me; and he that despiseth me despiseth him that sent me": Luke x. 16. "He that receiveth whomsoever I send, receiveth me; and he that receiveth me receiveth him that sent me*": John xiii. 20. The conclusion is obvious. Suppose that I find everything concerning baptism plainly revealed by the Apostles; suppose that, through a groundless association of ideas, or ignorance of the relation of the Old and New Testaments, I cannot explain some things in the

---

* As by proclaiming Jesus to be his beloved Son, and commanding men to hear him, the Father pledged himself for the truth of Christ's doctrine, so the Lord, by the commission he gave to his Apostles, pledged himself for the truth of whatever they taught.—H.

former Dispensation; ought I, or ought I not, to regulate my conduct by those whom Christ has chosen, qualified, commissioned, and sent to regulate it? You have anticipated the answer; but I repeat it in the words of the Apostle: " We (the Apostles) are of God; he that knoweth God heareth us : he that is not of God heareth not us. Hereby know we the spirit of truth and the spirit of error ": 1 John iv. 6.

V. *The Apostles were qualified and commissioned to explain the prophecies, types, and other mysteries of the Old Dispensation;* and they declare, and have confirmed the truth of the declaration by miracles, that they have faithfully, and as far as the interests of the Church required, completely executed this part of their commission. Men were miraculously qualified for explaining the mysteries of the Old Testament. " For to one is given by the Spirit the word of wisdom ; to another the word of knowledge by the same Spirit . . . . . to another prophecy ": 1 Cor. xii. 8, 10. Members of churches used these gifts for the edification of the churches to which they severally belonged. The Apostles possessed these gifts in a super-eminent degree, and committed their revelations to writing for the instruction of all the churches, in every age. Paul often speaks of this branch of his commission and work; for example, " If ye have heard of the dispensation of the grace of God which is given me to you-ward: how that by revelation he made known unto me the mystery ; (as I wrote afore in few words,) whereby, when ye read, ye may understand my knowledge in the mystery of Christ ".

Eph. iii. 3, 4. Repeating the same thing to the Colossians, he tells them, that he taught every man in all wisdom: Coloss. i. 25—28. Of the execution of this part of his work we have manifold examples. I name two or three: the antitype of Abraham's two wives, Sarah and Hagar; the meaning and antitype of circumcision; the marvellous revelations in the Epistle to the Hebrews. The clearness with which the Apostles executed this work, both absolute and comparative, they not only exemplify, but likewise declare. Take one example: "Seeing then that we have such hope, we use great plainness of speech; and not as Moses, which put a vail over his face, that the children of Israel could not stedfastly look to the end of that which is abolished: but their minds were blinded: for until this day remaineth the same vail untaken away in the reading of the Old Testament; which vail is done away in Christ. But even unto this day, when Moses is read, the vail is upon their heart": 2 Cor. iii. 12—15. And after referring to the faithfulness with which he fulfilled the ministry committed to him, the Apostle adds, "But if our Gospel be hid, it is hid to them that are lost, in whom the god of this world hath blinded the minds of them which believe not": 2 Cor. iv. 3, 4.

Mark now the proof which these things afford of our position, that the Scriptures of the New Testament are the only rule of the doctrine of the positive institutions of the Gospel Dispensation. Such as prefer to be guided by the Old Testament, ask how the Apostles, accustomed to the circumcision of infants, would understand their commission if it had run in these words: Go and teach all nations, circumcising them. They would have us look at the doctrine of the Apostles only through the medium of the law, or (as they generally express it) to carry the former state of things along with us. The facts just produced will enable the enquirer to answer the question. The Apostles were never in their *official* capacity left to inference, or to their own judgment. Whilst Christ was with them in the flesh, they baptized according to his instructions; and when he went to heaven, they delivered to the churches whatever, by the Holy Ghost, he was pleased to teach them. As to ourselves, we have their example, their doctrine, their expositions of the law, and, particularly, complete information respecting circumcision and baptism.

What is the conscientious inquirer now to do? Is he to judge by the mystery, or the explanation of the mystery? Is he to judge by the type, or the plain speech? Is he to examine the subject by the meridian light, or by the comparative darkness? Is he to look at the object through a vail, or with open face? If any man refuse to come to the light, if a man prefer the darkness before it, the Scriptures tell us the reason. The present subject illustrates this information. To darken the clear light of apostolical doctrine by clouds of groundless inferences, is not only preposterous, but sinful. The Apostles are the commissioned expositors of the law: they have executed their commission, as might be expected from men enlightened and directed by the Holy Ghost. To neglect their teaching for unwarranted imaginations of our own is highly presumptuous.

VI. *The Apostles declare, and by their miracles have proved the truth of their declaration, that they have executed their commission faithfully and completely.* " Let a man so account of us, as of the ministers of Christ, and stewards of the mysteries of God. Moreover it is required in stewards, that a man be found faithful ". Paul claims to have been faithful, and adds, "but he that judgeth me is the Lord" : 1 Cor. iv. 1, 2. " God hath made us able ministers of the New Testament " : 2 Cor. iii. 6. " I have not shunned to declare unto you all the counsel of God": Acts xx. 27. " These things write I unto thee . . that thou mayest know how thou oughtest to behave thyself in the house of God" : 1 Tim. iii. 14, 15. " For this cause left I thee in Crete, that thou shouldest set in order the things that are wanting, and ordain elders in every city, as *I* had appointed thee " : Titus i. 5.

They command all their institutions to be observed on pain of separation. " Therefore, brethren, stand fast, and hold the traditions which ye have been taught, whether by word, or our epistle " : 2 Thess. ii. 15. " Be ye followers of me, even as I also am of Christ. Now I praise you, brethren, that you remember me in all things, and keep the ordinances, as I delivered them unto you " : 1 Cor. xi. 1, 2. On occasion of a particular order Paul writes, " And *so* ordain I in all churches " : 1 Cor. vii. 17. " For this cause have I sent unto you Timotheus, who is my beloved son, and faithful in the Lord, who shall bring you into remembrance of *my ways* which be in Christ, *as I teach* everywhere in every church ": 1 Cor. iv. 17. " Now we command you, brethren, in the name of our Lord

Jesus Christ, that ye withdraw yourselves from every brother that walketh disorderly, and not after the tradition which he received of *us* ": 2 Thess. iii. 6.

This language is plain and conclusive, but there is a fact which exceedingly heightens the evidence. The primitive churches were, in general, richly furnished with miraculous gifts. We learn from the last chapter of the first epistle, that the church at Thessalonica enjoyed this distinction. The church of Corinth had prophets, teachers, and other spiritual men; men in possession of miraculous gifts, in great numbers, and of great distinction. Timothy and Titus were qualified and commissioned for extraordinary work, the work of evangelists. Yet it is not allowed to any, or to all who possessed miraculous gifts in any of the churches—it is not allowed to the evangelists themselves to increase, or diminish, or alter, in the smallest degree, any of the positive institutions of Christianity, as ordained by the Apostles. The consequence need hardly be mentioned. If it shall be found that the Apostles command us to baptize or sprinkle our infants, it is at our peril that we neglect to obey them. But if it shall be found that the Apostles have given no such instructions, I leave it to those who tremble at the word of the Lord, to judge of the temerity of the man who does, on the authority of some groundless imagination, that which neither the prophets, evangelists, nor spiritual men of the primitive churches might presume to attempt.

Our second position was, That the Scriptures of the New Testament are the only rule to direct us in the positive institutions of the Gospel Dispensation. In proof of this position, six reasons have been adduced. Each of them proves it, much more all of them taken together. Recollect that the Old Dispensation is come to an end—that the sacred writers call the Gospel a *new* Dispensation, in distinction from the old, and every branch of the Old Dispensation—that Christ is Lord of the New Dispensation—and that we are commanded to hear Him, in distinction from Moses and Elias—that the Apostles, exclusively, are commissioned to make known to the churches the laws of the kingdom of heaven,—that the Apostles were qualified and commissioned for the very purpose of explaining the Old Dispensation. Add to all this, that the Apostles have executed their commission faithfully and completely: they have put us in possession of the whole will of God respecting these institutions in general, and respecting baptism and all its parts, in particular. Take these things together, and the path of duty becomes plain. I must learn the institutions of the Gospel from the New Testament, and practise what I have thus learned.

This position is still farther confirmed by some general considerations, which come to be stated before I take leave of it. 1. Take the Old Testament altogether, from Genesis to Malachi, take the New Testament altogether, from Matthew to Revelation, then, let me ask, are we to regulate all the institutions of the latter, by all the institutions of the former, each by each; the elders, for example, of the New Testament by the priests of the Old—the materials of the churches, by the materials of the temple and tabernacle—the constitution of the churches of the one, by the constitution of the church of the other—baptism, by circumcision—the Lord's-supper, by the passover—the discipline of the last, by the discipline of the first Dispensation, and so on? If we are answered in the affirmative, where, then, it must be asked, do we receive our instructions for this procedure? And if such instructions can be found, why are they not, in all their extent, reduced to practice?

2. Should it be said that it is not by the Old Testament taken together, but by some particular branch of the Old Dispensation, that the institutions of the New Testament are to be regulated; we must inquire which branch is to be preferred? Not the Mosaic branch, say some, because circumcision "is not of Moses, but of the fathers": John vii. 22. The text alluded to is misunderstood, or misapplied; but waiving the mistake, the question returns, Which branch is to be preferred? There are three branches before the Mosaic. The first, from Adam to Noah; the second, from Noah to Abraham; the third, from Abraham to Moses. The motive for preferring the Abrahamic branch is obvious. Should we take the first branch, or the second, neither parents nor children were circumcised; and on the principles of Pædo-baptists, there would be no baptism either of parents or of their infants. Still, however, a reason must be asked for the preference,— and it must be farther asked,—Are all the institutions of the Gospel to be regulated by all the institutions of the Abrahamic covenant? If in one thing only the Gospel is to be ruled by that law, a reason must be assigned for this singularity. But, suppose all these difficulties surmounted,

(which the inquirer will find to be impracticable)—suppose for a moment that circumcision is to regulate the administration of baptism, a new series of unanswerable questions immediately present themselves. Where is the law obliging us to regulate baptism by circumcision? And, suppose the law produced—(which cannot be done)—is the law of circumcision, in all its parts, or in one particular only, to regulate the ordinance of baptism? If, in one particular only, where is this law of peculiarity? If, in all its parts, why is not the principle acted on in all its extent? Why are not females excluded from baptism, as they were by the Abrahamic covenant from circumcision? Why is not the eighth day exclusively observed? Why are not servants baptized on the faith of their masters, and adults in a family on the faith of their parent?

The fact is, that neither Papist, Episcopalian, Presbyterian, nor Pædo-baptist acts on his own principles. Christianity has been corrupted on a false principle, and the principle is inconsistently defended for the sake of the consequences of the corruption. The candid inquirer, on reflecting on these things, can hardly fail to be satisfied, that had it not been for a groundless association of ideas, he would never have seriously listened to arguments for infant-baptism founded on the laws of the Old Dispensation.

He will search the New Testament, and by what he finds there will regulate his principles and practice, notwithstanding his inability to free himself at once and completely from the influence of long cherished prejudice.

LECTURE IV.

OUR PRACTICE MUST BE DETERMINED BY THOSE PASSAGES OF SCRIPTURE WHICH MORE DIRECTLY TREAT OF THE SUBJECT OF INQUIRY.

Position III. Those passages of Scripture which treat of baptism more directly and more fully, must determine our judgment, in distinction from such passages as refer to the subject more indirectly, or not at all.

This position needs no proof; it shines in its own light. In the New Testament there are many passages which fully and directly treat of baptism, there are some which merely refer to it, and many which do not refer to it at all. One would expect that in directing the student in his enquiries concerning baptism, teachers would follow the course which common sense suggests; that they would recommend special attention to those passages which directly and fully treat on the subject, and would advise the student to form his judgment by them. The reverse of this, however, has been, and still is the plan followed by the teachers of Pædo-baptism.

When our Lord commissioned the Apostles to evangelize the nations, he gave them particular instructions on the subject of baptism. Matt.

xxviii. 19. The manner in which they executed their instructions is exemplified in a great variety of instances. I shall quote some of them. "Then Peter said unto them, Repent, and be baptized every one of you in the name of Jesus Christ for the remission of sins, and ye shall receive the gift of the Holy Ghost. . . . . Then they that gladly received his word were baptized ": Acts ii. 38, 41. "But when they believed Philip preaching the things concerning the kingdom of God, and the name of Jesus Christ, they were baptized, both men and women": Acts viii. 12. "And as they went on their way, they came unto a certain water: and the eunuch said, See, here is water; what doth hinder me to be baptized? And Philip said, If thou believest with all thine heart, thou mayest. And he answered and said, I believe that Jesus Christ is the Son of God. And he commanded the chariot to stand still; and they went down both into the water, both Philip and the eunuch; and he baptized him": verses 36—38. "And immediately there fell from his eyes as it had been scales: and he received sight forthwith, and arose, and was baptized": Acts ix. 18. "Can any man forbid water, that these should not be baptized, which have received the Holy Ghost as well as we? And he commanded them to be baptized in the name of the Lord": Acts x. 47, 48. "And when she was baptized, and her household, she besought us, saying, If ye have judged me to be faithful to the Lord, come into my house, and abide there. And she constrained us": Acts xvi. 15. "And he took them the same hour of the night, and washed their stripes; and was baptized, he and all his, straightway . . . . believing in God with all his house:" verses 33, 34. "And Crispus, the chief ruler of the synagogue, believed on the Lord with all his house; and many of the Corinthians hearing believed, and were baptized": Acts xviii. 8.

In these scriptures the subject is fully and distinctly taught. But is it to these, or scriptures like these, that the teachers of Pædo-baptism direct our attention? Quite otherwise. For proof of infant-baptism, we are directed to passages which speak of baptism, *but not of infants;* or which speak of infants, *but not of baptism;* and often to scriptures which speak *neither of infants nor baptism.* That a course so preposterous should be either adopted or encouraged, nothing but the fact could persuade us to believe. Yet such the fact unquestionably is; and it may, therefore, be useful to quote the scriptures offered in evidence of infant baptism.

We are now on the subject of evidence; and the mere quotation of the scriptures referred to will satisfy the candid inquirer that it is not from such, but from scriptures which expressly treat of the subject, that he must form his judgment on the doctrine of baptism. "Then were there brought unto him little children, that he should put his hands on them, and pray: and the disciples rebuked them. But Jesus said, Suffer little children, and forbid them not, to come unto me: for of such is the kingdom of heaven. And he laid his hands on them, and departed thence": Matt. xix. 13. Here is mention of infants, and the kingdom of heaven; but no mention of their admission to baptism.

They were brought, not to be baptized, but that our Lord should put his hands on them, and pray. He did not baptize them; he laid his hands on them, and departed thence.

The next in order is Acts ii. 39: "For the promise is unto you, and to your children, and to all that are afar off, even as many as the Lord our God shall call". Here is mention of *children*, and a promise; but none of *infants, or their baptism*. The word children is here taken in the sense of descendants, of age sufficient for prophesying and being called. Their capacity for prophesying appears from comparing with the text the prediction quoted by Peter: Acts ii. 17-31. You will find it in Joel ii. 28-32. That these descendants were capable of being called appears from the text. "For the promise is unto you and to your children, and to all that are afar off, [Infants? Nay,] even as many as the Lord our God shall call". Therefore I said, here is no mention of infants, or of the baptism of infants; but if the inquirer examine the whole context, he will find that men, after gladly receiving the word, ought to be baptized, and that infants ought not to be baptized.

We are next referred to Acts xvi., for the baptism of the household of Lydia and of the jailor. But in this chapter not a word occurs of either the baptism or the sprinkling of infants.

The scripture next adduced is Rom. iv. 11: "And he received the sign of circumcision, a seal of the righteousness of the faith which he had yet being uncircumcised." The Apostle is here treating of justification without the works of the law;

and in proof of his doctrine, he refers to the history of Abraham and his circumcision. He does not mention either infants or baptism.

In Galatians iii. 29, it is written, "If ye be Christ's, then are ye Abraham's seed, and heirs according to the promise." It is evident from the context, that by "Abraham's seed" is meant, partakers of like precious faith with Abraham. This passage cannot, therefore, apply to infants.

Rom. xi. 16: "For if the firstfruit be holy, the lump is also holy: and if the root be holy, so are the branches." This is another example of pleading for infant baptism from a text treating neither of infants, nor of sprinkling, nor of baptism. The apostle is treating of the conversion of the Jews, and the figures refer to them and the patriarchs.*

1 Cor. vii. 14: "For the unbelieving husband is sanctified by the wife, and the unbelieving wife is sanctified by the husband; else were your children unclean, but now are they holy." The Corinthians had consulted Paul whether a believing husband might live with an unbelieving spouse. He acquaints them with the law on the subject, which

---

* Abraham, the friend of God, is represented as the root from which the branches (his descendants) were broken off. While the Lord admits that the unbelieving Jews were Abraham's seed, (John viii. 37,) he denies that they were the children of Abraham, ver. 39. This honourable title belongs only to those who are Christ's: Gal. iii. 29. The Jews were broken off because of unbelief, and they shall be graffed in again by faith: Rom. xi. 23. At present, Abraham does not acknowledge them (Is. lxiii. 16); nor will he do so till they shall "look on him whom they have pierced, and they shall mourn for him, as one mourneth for his only son, and shall be in bitterness for him, as one that is in bitterness for his firstborn."—Zech. xii. 10.— J. H.

sanctified the relation. He is not treating of baptism, nor does he mention, in any way, the sprinkling of infants.

Eph. vi. 1—5: "Children, obey your parents in the Lord, for this is right. Honour thy father and mother, which is the first commandment with promise, that it may be well with thee, and thou mayest live long on the earth. And, ye fathers, provoke not your children to wrath, but bring them up in the nurture and admonition of the Lord Servants, be obedient to them that are your masters according to the flesh." In this paragraph we have children, but not infants. The children are capable of receiving *this address*, and of judging what commands of their parents were, or were not, in the Lord. And let it be particularly observed, that children are addressed on the same ground on which servants are addressed, namely, their relation to Christ, and not on the ground of grace derived by them either from their parents or masters. If these addresses prove that children ought to be baptized or sprinkled on account of their connection with their parents, they also prove that servants ought to be baptized on account of their connection with their masters. But the fact is, that the apostle is not treating of baptism, nor speaking of the baptism or sprinkling either of infants or of servants. To save time, I omit similar exhortations to children and servants, although they have been used in argument by Pædo-baptists, for the remarks just made apply to them all.

Col. ii. 10—13: "And ye are complete in him, which is the head of all principality and power; in whom also ye are circumcised with the circumcision made without hands, in putting off the body of the sins of the flesh by the circumcision of Christ; buried with him in baptism, wherein also ye are risen with him, through the faith of the operation of God, who hath raised him from the dead: and you, being dead in your sins and the uncircumcision of your flesh, hath he quickened together with him, having forgiven you all trespasses". In these words we have baptism, but no infants. The Colossians are described as "saints and faithful brethren in Christ"; and in this place, as believers, both justified and sanctified. Observe, they possess "faith of the operation of God", God has forgiven them all their trespasses; they have "the circumcision of Christ, the circumcision made without hands," namely, "the putting off the body of the sins of the flesh." It will be recollected that it is with facts, and not with inferences, that we are at present concerned. The apostle, in this place, speaks nothing of infants. His object is to dissuade the Colossians from subjecting themselves to the institutions of philosophy, or of the law. He tells them, that having believed in Christ, they were complete—justified and sanctified; and that their union with Christ and their participation in these benefits were signified in their baptism. The whole is an example, not of the baptism of infants, but of the necessity of regeneration and of faith in those who are baptized.

These are all the passages in the New Testament which, as far as I know, have been pleaded in support of infant baptism. None of them are pertinent; in every one of them there is wanting something essential to make it conclusive. Minds practised in reasoning must be satisfied already that infant baptism cannot be admitted on evidence like this. According to the position before us, it must be received or rejected on the scriptures which treat of the subjects of baptism. An example may assist the young in reaching the same conviction. Suppose that, by a deed of entail, an estate was conveyed in succession to the eldest male in a certain lineage: suppose that an action for obtaining the estate is raised: suppose, farther, that the applicant is either not of the line described in the deed of entail, or not the eldest in the line, or a female: the rejection of the plea must necessarily follow. Yet this is the very kind of evidence on which infant baptism has been defended and practised. We have examined all the passages adduced. Some of them speak of infants, but nothing of baptism; all of them, we have seen, are palpably deficient in the proof required.

The importance and evidence of this position require me, before I pass to another, to press the consideration of it on my readers, from their sense of consistency.

We have discontinued the observance of the seventh-day Sabbath; but improperly, if the arguments for infant baptism be correct. The New Testament, indeed, says that no man ought to judge us in respect of a Sabbath; but apply the arguments for sprinkling, and, according to them, we shall find that, notwithstanding this, and similar texts, we must still sanctify the seventh day of the week. In the epistle referred to, the apostle is reasoning on the doctrine of justification. The fourth commandment is not merely ceremonial, it stands in the first table of the decalogue. It is ranked with precepts moral and immutable : it was not of Moses, it was of the Fathers. It was more, it was before the fall; it was observed in Eden, in innocence, and sanctioned by the example of its Author. Spread out these topics, and the plea becomes plausible, incomparably more plausible than the plea for infant baptism. But what has been the conduct of the professing world in regard to the seventh day, and on what principles has that conduct been adopted and pursued? The observance of the seventh-day Sabbath has been discontinued. The grounds of the change are, shortly, two: first, The Old Dispensation is at an end; secondly, The scriptures of the New Testament, which more fully treat of the Lord's-day, direct us to the first day of the week. This is the doctrine of our position; and the man who determines the first day of the week to be the day of worship, is bound, in consistency, also to determine, upon the same principle, who shall be the subjects of baptism.

Permit me, by one example more, to illustrate and enforce my position. In this and other countries, originally connected with the Papacy, *infants have been excluded from communion.* This exclusion is scriptural: infants ought not to be admitted to the Lord's Table. *But admit them we must, on the pleas by which infant baptism is justified.* The pleas for baptizing infants, and admitting them to the Supper, are the same : point for point they agree; together they must be admitted as conclusive, or together rejected as sophistical. Let us run the parallel, and make the experiment. Does baptism come in the place of circumcision ? By the same kind of evidence the Supper comes in place of the passover. Were children circumcised? Children likewise partook of the festal sacrifices, and most evidently of the passover. Was circumcision before the law, and of the Fathers? So were sacrifices: the passover, in particular, was instituted in Egypt previous to the covenant at Sinai. Is the same truth represented by baptism and circumcision ? Both the Supper and the passover exhibit the sacrifice of Christ. Must the former state of things, that is, circumcision, determine the subjects of baptism ? For the same reason, the former state of things, that is, the passover, must determine the subjects of the Supper. Children belong to the kingdom of heaven. If this privilege proves infant baptism, it proves also infant communion. Many prophecies connect parents with their seed. If these prophecies prove that infants should be baptized, they prove also that infants should be admitted to the Supper. The promise is to the Israelites, and to their children : if this warrants the baptism of infants, it warrants also their communion. The root and the branches are holy : if this establishes either infant baptism or infant communion, it establishes both. Children of believers are holy: the holiness that qualifies for Baptism, qualifies as effectually for the Supper. Households were baptized: every one knows that the passover was eaten by households. Is the practice of baptizing infants of remote antiquity? Infant communion was as ancient as pædo-baptism, and much more ancient than sprinkling. Have pædo-baptism and sprinkling been practised by men of learning and piety? Infant communion has a like recommendation.

It is objected to infant communion, that infants can neither examine themselves, nor eat the Supper in remembrance of Christ. Against infant baptism there lies a similar objection. Infants can perform no baptismal duties, either antecedent, concomitant, or consequent. To the objection against infant baptism, it is answered, that faith, confessing the faith, and other baptismal duties, must be restricted to the adult, like the command which restricts eating to working, for the apostle could never have intended that an infant shall not eat because he does not work. The answer is equally applicable to the objection against infant communion. It is as absurd to require his faith to his communion, as his work to his sustenance, or his confession to his baptism.

On what grounds, let me now ask, ought infant communion to be rejected? On two, it will be answered: first, the Old Dispensation is at an end; and secondly, the Apostles' doctrine in its obvious sense restricts this communion to believers. But this is our position again, and again I repeat the consequence,—the man who by this rule determines the subjects of the Supper, is in consistency bound also to determine the subjects of baptism in like manner.

The sum of what has been said is this:—The scriptures which treat on the subject, and not other scriptures, must determine the question of baptism. It is on this principle that men proceed in determining other questions, and the advocates of infant baptism reverse the practice in this one case only. We have produced two examples (out of many) of the way in which Pædo-baptists act upon the principle which we have laid down, namely, their discontinuance of infant communion and their observance of the seventh-day sabbath. In those instances, the position, that we are to be guided by those passages which more directly treat of the subject of inquiry, is acted on; and deductions and inferences from passages which do not relate to the subject are quite abandoned. Thus the foundation of the grandest argument for infant baptism is reprobated by the professing world in general, and is practically abandoned by Pædo-baptists themselves in other matters.

Another stage, then, of the inquirer's road is made plain: he will, depending on Divine teaching, collect and examine all the passages of the New Testament which treat of baptism, and by them will determine all the questions which surround this subject.

LECTURE V.

POSITIVE PROOF ESSENTIAL TO WORSHIP IN BAPTISM.

Position IV. Proof in some degree positive is essential to worship in Baptism.

Before I can take part in baptizing an infant, either as administrator or sponsor, I must be satisfied that the action is positively required, and I cannot rest satisfied with a mere notion that, peradventure, it may be my duty. We have been so long accustomed to hear infant baptism defended by certain arguments, that we are apt to believe that there may be something in them, although we cannot tell what. On this undefined feeling, without further evidence, many take part in the practice, and decline being themselves baptized. They reason thus: "Although I cannot find them, there may be examples of infant baptism; and, although I am not satisfied with the arguments for the practice, there may be something in them. I know not why, but I feel a suspicion, that the Baptists *must* be wrong; for the present, I will delay my own baptism; and as to my child, I will proceed as usual". Now, if our position be true, this apology is inadmissible, and the conduct founded on it is wrong.

1. In proof that evidence in some degree positive is essential to worship in baptism, I observe, first, that *the formula commonly used runs*

in positive terms; and without some degree of positive evidence I cannot conscientiously use it. The words of the formula are, " I baptize thee in the name ", which means, amongst other things, I baptize thee by the commandment of God. The words are not—I baptize thee, perhaps or it may be, by the command of God. The words mean, that there is a command for baptizing infants; that I know that there is such a command; and that I act on the positive knowledge that there is. Now, unless there be such a command, and unless it consist with my knowledge that there is, I cannot conscientiously act under the formula. I prevaricate, when I intimate that I know it, when I only imagine that possibly there may be such a command. Suppose that a prisoner is indicted for murder, committed at such a time, in such a place; suppose that a witness depones that the prisoner committed the deed at the time and in the place indicated; suppose, farther, on cross-examination, he admits that he cannot positively say whether the accused was in the place at the time; or that he committed the deed; but that his (the witness's) mind was impressed, he could not well tell how, that the prisoner might have been in the place at the time mentioned, and that, perhaps, he committed the murder. In a case like this, few need to be told that the counsel for the accused would not fail to remind the jury that this witness had prevaricated on oath. Most assuredly neither judge nor jury would pay the least attention to his evidence.

I use the example, not to measure the degree of criminality, but to illustrate and establish the fact that the man prevaricates—whether as administrator or sponsor, who, without some degree of positive proof that he is doing right, takes part in baptizing a child in the name of the Trinity.

2. Proof in some degree positive is essential, because *faith is essential to worship in baptism.* The necessity of faith in every part of worship is often and plainly asserted. "Without faith it is impossible to please God". "Whatsoever is not of faith is sin". The necessity of positive evidence to faith may, without difficulty, be evinced. "Faith cometh . . . . by the word of God": Rom. x. 17. Unless a fact be revealed, and I know that it is revealed, I cannot believe it. I do not believe, if I suppose only that perhaps it is revealed. "He that cometh to God must believe that He is, and that He is the rewarder of them that diligently seek him". The acceptable worshipper must be persuaded, not that there may be a God, but that there is a God: not that perhaps he may, but that he will, reward them who diligently seek him. He that believes that Jesus is the Christ—not he that supposes that perhaps Jesus is the Christ—shall be saved. Apply these things to infant baptism. *If it be not practised in faith, it is sin.*

To faith in any divine truth, two things are required; first, that it be revealed in the Scriptures; and, secondly, that I know that it is revealed. As yet I inquire not whether it be or be not revealed; but suppose, either that it is not revealed, or that I do not know that it is: it cannot be practised in faith. If I imagine merely that peradventure it may be revealed, this is not faith; and therefore during this uncertainty of mind, I cannot with a good conscience take any part in the practice, either as administrator or sponsor. "Happy is he that condemneth not himself in that thing which he alloweth. And he that doubteth is condemned if he eat, because he eateth not of faith; for whatsoever is not of faith is sin": Rom. xiv. 22, 23. "Let every man be fully persuaded in his own mind": Rom. xiv. 5.

3. Proof in some degree positive is essential in baptism, because *without such proof our service would be will-worship*. We are guilty of will-worship when we worship without a warrant from Scripture. "To the law and to the testimony: if they speak not according to this word, it is because there is no light in them": Isaiah viii. 20. "To worship without a warrant, without evidence, and without certainty, are sins of the same kind; if they differ, they differ only in degree: the guilt of will-worship more or less attaches to them all. To worship without knowing the warrant is, as to the worshipper, as though no warrant existed; and to act in uncertainty, is to act on a peradventure that there may be no warrant. What may be, may also not be; to act, therefore, under uncertainty whether I have or have not a warrant for my conduct, is to act under uncertainty whether I am or am not contracting the guilt of will-worship; and in such a case I do in some degree contract that guilt.

Suppose that an apothecary kills a patient by selling him poison instead of medicine; suppose it proved on his trial that the apothecary knew the drug to be poison, he would be guilty of death; he had murdered his patient. Supposing it proved that he sold the poison suspecting it might be poison; a question might arise among the jurors respecting the designation of his crime—whether he should be found guilty of murder, or of culpable homicide. But, whatever name they may give to his crime, acquit him they could not: he had criminally taken away the life of his patient.

If, under a conviction that I have no Scripture warrant for my conduct, I take part in baptizing a child, I contract the guilt of will-worship, in all its malignity: if I act under a conviction that, for any thing I know, it may be will-worship, the degree may be less, but my sin is the same in kind; still I am guilty of will-worship.

We are now prepared to state and answer the practical question,—May I, in the circumstances supposed, without some degree of positive assurance that it is required of me, take part in baptizing or sprinkling my child? I may not; in the fear of God I cannot proceed. The doctrine of Scripture here is plain and often repeated. "Ye hypocrites, well did Esaias prophesy of you, saying, ... In vain do they worship me, teaching for doctrines the commandments of men": Matt. xv. 7—9. "Be not ye called Rabbi: for one is your Master, even Christ; and all ye are brethren. And call no man your father upon the earth: for one is your Father, which is in heaven. Neither be ye called masters: for one is your Master, even Christ": Matt. xxiii. 8—10. "Wherefore, if ye be dead with Christ from the rudiments of the world, why, as though living in the world, are ye subject to ordinances . . after the commandments and doctrines of men?" Col. ii. 20, 22.

4. Evidence, in some degree positive or real, is

POSITIVE PROOF ESSENTIAL. 51

essential to worship in baptism, because, *acting without this kind of evidence, I am guilty of offending my brother*. To offend, is to tempt to sin. Offences are often given in many ways. In the case before us, I give offence when I tempt another to perform an action, of the lawfulness of which he is not fully satisfied. A good conscience requires that, in his own mind, the agent have no doubt of the lawfulness of his conduct. Some Gentile converts questioned the lawfulness of eating things offered to idols; some Jewish converts questioned the propriety of eating meats forbidden by Moses; for such to eat—in violation of their scruples—was to sin, perhaps to destruction. To tempt them to eat was to offend them; it was to lay a stumblingblock in their way, over which they might fall into sin and perdition. The doctrine before us is both illustrated and proved by these plain and pointed references. If my evidence of infant baptism does not exceed a "peradventure," a "may be" that it is lawful, I cannot but doubt; and he that doubteth is condemned. If my brother imitate my practice, that is, if he act, whilst he has scruples about the lawfulness of his conduct, he falls under the same condemnation. I, in the meantime, am doubly guilty; I am self-condemned, because I doubt the lawfulness of my own procedure; I offend my brother, and make his guilt and danger my own. The language of Scripture on this subject is peculiarly striking. "Take heed, lest by any means this liberty of yours become a stumblingblock to them that are weak. For if any man see thee which hast knowledge sit at meat in the idol's temple, shall not the conscience of him which is weak be emboldened to eat those things which are offered to idols; and through thy knowledge shall the weak brother perish, for whom Christ died? But when ye sin so against the brethren, and wound their weak conscience, ye sin against Christ. Wherefore, if meat make my brother to offend, I will eat no flesh while the world standeth, lest I make my brother to offend": 1 Cor. viii. 9—13. "Let us not, therefore, judge one another any more: but judge this rather, that no man put a stumblingblock or an occasion to fall in his brother's way. . . . To him that esteemeth any thing to be unclean, to him it is unclean. . . For meat destroy not the work of God. All things indeed are pure; but it is evil for that man who eateth with offence. It is good neither to eat flesh, nor to drink wine, nor any thing whereby thy brother stumbleth, or is offended, or is made weak," &c.: Rom. xiv. 13, 14, 20, 21. "Woe unto the world because of offences! for it must be that offences come; but woe to that man by whom the offence cometh": Matt. xviii. 7.

Here, before we proceed farther, it may be proper to apply the remarks already made. Everyone knows, or may know, the grounds and character of his own convictions; and according to them he ought to continue, or decline to take part, in baptizing or sprinkling infants. Conduct, in every man of principle, must be determined by the dictates of his conscience.* If he find that the

---

* We may, however, through ignorance, put good for evil, and evil for good; the strength of our conviction will not justify any improper practice, but if we sin against our conviction, we act presumptuously.—J. H.

practice is groundless, he must renounce it, for the same reason that human authority must be renounced in other matters of religion. If he have doubts, he cannot proceed, for he that doubteth is condemned. If he be conscious that his convictions do not rise above a peradventure, or may be, his practice cannot be of faith, and whatever is not of faith is sin.

There are two other classes of professors who should here be addressed. The first of these float on the tide of fashion: they have never inquired, and have no intention of inquiring after truth. These may have no doubts, but they can have no faith. In words, perhaps, they call no man master; but, knowing no warrant for it, their practice is will-worship. They may not intend either to profane the name of God, or offend their brethren; yet they do both. They abuse the common formula, and by their inconsiderate conduct tempt others to imitate their profanity. They shut their eyes against the light, and their ears against the voice of God in the Scriptures calling them to inquire. They have already reached the borders of presumptuous sinning; before they pass them, it is their interest to pause. "To him that knoweth to do good, and doeth it not, to him it is sin".

The class which comes next to be considered, consists of those who really believe in the doctrine of infant baptism. It is a fact, that error or mistake may be as confidently credited and defended as truth. Transubstantiation was introduced into the church in the thirteenth century; for six hundred years it has formed an article in the Romish creed. Protestants have often, and unanswerably, proved it to be idolatrous and absurd. The priests, however, have all along defended the absurdity, and the people have approved of their sophistry. Light and learning have greatly increased, yet transubstantiation continues the disgrace of the reason and consciences of men. Amidst all the improvements of the nineteenth century, the monstrous tenet is, throughout the wide extent of the Papacy, defended and believed with unabating confidence. This is a mortifying but instructive fact. Infant baptism has been defended by men who professed to believe it. Multitudes have been, and still are, misled by their apparent sincerity; but neither the reasonings of men, however confidently urged, nor their belief, however sincere, is the rule of our conduct. Confident assertions have been mistaken for evidence; but our appeal must be to the Scriptures of Truth. Notwithstanding the numbers, and the confidence with which they have been defended, transubstantiation and infant baptism may both be corruptions of Christianity. "To the law and to the testimony; if they speak not according to this word, it is because there is no light in them."

The fact that error is often believed with confidence, is equally instructive to believers in infant baptism and transubstantiation. Was pædo-baptism silently and gradually introduced into the Church? so comparatively was transubstantiation. Is pædo-baptism of great antiquity? transubstantiation has prevailed for 600 years. Has pædo-baptism been supported by learning? so has transubstantiation. Has sprinkling been defended with plausibility? the words, "this is my body," applied to the bread, give a plea to the Papists more plausible than any that has yet been urged in defence of infant baptism. Has infant baptism hitherto survived the attacks of its opponents? transubstantiation exists, nothwithstanding all the labours of the Reformed. Are Pædo-baptists confident in their cause? so are the Papists. Do Pædo-baptists exult in their numbers? so do the abettors of transubstantiation. The parallel proceeds; but I follow it no farther than to its application. What is the duty of the Papist as to transubstantiation? I answer,—the same as the duty of the believer in infant baptism. Both the one and the other ought by the Scriptures to examine the grounds of his confidence. "For not he that commendeth himself is approved, but whom the Lord commendeth."

Before concluding, it may be useful to exemplify the more particular application of our position.

It has been disputed on whom lies what logicians call the *onus probandi*. The *onus probandi*, that is, the labour of finding warrant for our practice, lies on the man who practises infant baptism. Every Pædo-baptist, if he would act in the fear of God, must furnish himself with satisfactory evidence that God requires it at his hands. By satisfactory, I understand what has been proved; not that for any thing he knows, it may be so; but that, from Scripture, he is convinced in his own conscience that infant baptism is an ordinance of God.

That we may more clearly see how to apply this position to practice, I shall take a case of common occurrence. The inquirer has an infant: he deliberates whether it be his duty to have it baptized, or to delay baptism until the gospel be credibly professed; he will, and perhaps not improperly, have recourse to the arguments for sprinkling. A hint to such may be useful.

In perusing every particular argument, mark down all the Scriptures offered in proof. Lay aside your author; and examine the proof scriptures in the Bible itself, in *their connection*. After prayer and consideration, judge, as you must answer at the last day, whether these Scriptures, in the connection in which they stand in the Bible, satisfy your conscience that God requires you to baptize or sprinkle your child.

In looking into the fire, or at the clouds, you sometimes observe something like figures—birds, beasts, men, and the like. These figures, every one knows, are the effect of imagination working on certain appearances in the clouds or in the fire; in a short time the appearances cease to exist. Texts, *taken out of their connection in the Bible*, and stuck into a well-wrought argument, may assume the appearance of evidence. Look at them in their connection in the Bible; and the evidence, like figures in the fire or the clouds, will speedily vanish. For a man wishing to tamper with his understanding, I know few rules more efficacious than never to look at the text adduced in proof, in the Bible, but always in some book that pleads for the favoured practice. The candid inquirer will follow a different course; he will examine the texts as they stand in the Scriptures; and until he find, to the satisfaction of his conscience, that it is an ordinance of God, he will take no part, directly or indirectly, in the practice of baptizing or sprinkling infants.

LECTURE VI.

ESTIMATE OF THE VALUE OF INFERENTIAL REASONING ON THE SUBJECT OF BAPTISM.

The opponents of infant-sprinkling have generally objected to inferential reasoning on this topic. They distinguish between positive institutions and moral duties: the latter *may*, in their judgment; the former *cannot*, be admitted on inference. The abettors of the practice reply, "If the will of God be intimated, we are bound by the intimation, however made. Our duty is the same, whether intimated in express doctrine, or implied inference." The examination of these statements belongs to the head of evidence, and must now be attempted. At present, I confine my observations to the inquiry, Whether infant-sprinkling be rightly inferred from the topics usually adduced?

These topics may be reduced to three classes:— First, The procedure of professing Christians; Secondly, Certain texts in the Scriptures; Thirdly, Certain institutions once observed, but now discontinued by Divine appointment.

I. *The procedure of Pædo-baptists furnishes what has the appearance of evidence in their favour.* Multitudes have practised sprinkling; many have avowed their conviction that it is founded on argument; and not a few have defended the practice. These things, taken separately or together, assume, as I said, the appearance of evidence. If numbers so great have examined the question with capacity and integrity, it is probable that their practice is right, and their verdict true; and on this inference there is no doubt that many have sprinkled their children. Let us try this inference. Many are incapable, from ignorance and inattention, of examining or investigating the controversies on the subject; more, through indolence, have never examined them. Many are prejudiced, interested, and faithless. It is, therefore, no breach of charity to say that the testimony of such characters as these is not to be depended on. Notwithstanding their numbers, the Heathen, Mahommedan, and Papal worlds are wrong; and from anything that can be learned from their procedure, the infant-sprinkling world may be wrong also. The presumption is against them. Look at the generality of Pædo-baptist churches, Papal, Episcopalian, and Presbyterian; whoever has studied ecclesiastical polity will soon observe, that in reference to other institutions, the laws of Christ are not observed by these churches. The *unreserved* obedience of the Bible is a thing unknown to many of these societies.

This ought to put the inquirer on his guard. The prevarication of a witness in one point vitiates the whole of his evidence. If in other parts of ecclesiastical polity the Scriptures be disregarded, perhaps they are disregarded in the sprinkling of infants also. In all the defences of infant sprinkling, with few (if any) exceptions, violence is offered to the Scriptures. The simple rule for learning the mind of the Spirit is this:—"Collect whatever He has said on the subject in question, and by the collection regulate your faith." Instead, however, of collecting whatever the Spirit has revealed on baptism, the most explicit revelations are carefully avoided, and the reader is decoyed in another direction. The obvious meaning and design of particular texts are concealed, and inferences sometimes deduced from them directly the reverse of both. These things may leave us in doubt whether the authors are designing or mistaken; but they can leave us in no doubt respecting the character of their evidence. When a scholar tells us that sprinkling is baptism, and proves it from the eighth chapter of the Acts; when a logician infers baptism from circumcision, and proves his inference from the seventeenth chapter of Genesis; when a critic proves the sprinkling of infants from Luke's history of the baptism of such as gladly heard Peter's sermon, or from the seventh chapter of the first epistle to the Corinthians; and the inquirer allows himself to be misled by such testimony, he has himself to blame, and not those whom he has taken for his guides.

These remarks cannot be misunderstood. They are necessary for the sake of a part of the community peculiarly valuable. Christians, humble and teachable, have been, and will be, in danger of resigning their own better judgment to the prejudices and presumption of mistaken or designing men. Papists, Episcopalians, Presbyterians, and Independents, are generally Pædo-baptists. If, however, their procedure and defences be compared with the Scriptures, the contradiction will soon strike the studious inquirer, and by the Divine blessing preserve him from the influence of human examples however numerous and imposing.

Should a humble and modest Christian, unassisted by a liberal education, begin to examine the ground of infant baptism, he is commonly assailed with this observation:—" Many worthies, renowned for piety, talent, and learning, have practised and defended the popular worship. You are unlearned, weak, and inexperienced; it is presumptuous in you to question their evidence, or oppose your judgment to theirs." The facts just stated make this conclusion doubtful; but the Scriptures entirely reject such a principle. The individual is commanded to judge and act for himself; the Scriptures exclusively are prescribed as his rule; his duty is there stated and enforced, in terms negative and positive, often and plainly, and in great variety of language. " Search the Scriptures; for in them ye think ye have eternal life: and they are they which testify of me": John v. 39. "All Scripture is given by inspiration of God, and is profitable for doctrine, for reproof, for correction, for instruction in righteousness; that the man of God (every believer) may be perfect, throughly furnished unto all good works"; and consequently to the right observance of baptism: 2 Tim. iii. 16. " Prove all things; hold fast that which is good": 1 Thess. v. 21. The matter in question is infant baptism; the agent is every believer; the rule is the Scriptures; the result— hold or reject it according to this rule. And, to quote but one Scripture more, namely, Rev. iii. 22: " He that hath an ear, let him hear what the Spirit saith unto the churches". Thus it appears, that this popular inference is nothing more than a vulgar error. In no way can it justify infant sprinkling. The Scriptures themselves must be examined. If our faculties be impaired through inaction, more prayer and energy will be requisite. In the mean time, the practice, in as far as it is founded on this inference, must be discontinued. It is from God, and not from men, that we must take our instructions; it is from the Scriptures, and not from the works of men, that we must learn the will of God. Faith comes not by the reasonings of men, but by the word of God; and whatever is not of faith is sin.

II. The second ground of inference comprehends *the texts from which inferences are deduced.* I shall now name them together, and it will appear, from a few remarks on them, that the doctrine of infant baptism can be inferred from none of them. " Then were there brought unto him little children, that he should put his hands on them, and pray: and the disciples rebuked them" : Matt. xix. 13. " For the promise is unto you, and to your children, and to all that are afar off, even as many as the Lord our God shall call " : Acts ii. 39. " And when she was baptized, and her household, she besought us, saying, If ye have judged me to be faithful to the Lord, come into my house, and abide there. And she constrained us " : Acts xvi. 15. " And he took them the same hour of the night, and washed their stripes ; and was baptized, he and all his, straightway " : Acts xvi. 33. " And he received the sign of circumcision, a seal of the righteousness of the faith which he had yet being uncircumcised : that he might be the father of all them that believe, though they be not circumcised; that righteousness might be imputed unto them also": Rom. iv. 11. "For if the first-fruit be holy, the lump is also holy: and if the root be holy, so are the branches": Rom. xi. 16. "And I baptized also the household of Stephanas: besides, I know not whether I baptized any other": 1 Cor. i. 16. "For the unbelieving husband is sanctified by the wife, and the unbelieving wife is sanctified by the husband: else were your children unclean; but now are they holy": 1 Cor. vii. 14. "Children, obey your parents in the Lord; for this is right": Eph. vi. 1. "In whom also ye are circumcised with the circumcision made without hands, in putting off the body of the sins of the flesh by the circumcision of Christ": Col. ii. 11. And some have added John iii. 5: "Jesus answered, Verily, verily, I say unto you, Except a man be born of water and of the Spirit, he cannot enter into the kingdom of God".

These are all the texts quoted by Pædo-baptists in support of their practice. Not one is omitted that I can recollect. They were briefly commented on in a preceding lecture. They are now brought together, that the impression of their united force may be felt. Whatever in the contexts has a tendency to weaken the effect, has been intentionally suppressed. And now every individual must judge of the impression made on himself. I am greatly mistaken if any considerable number feel convinced by these texts that infant sprinkling is the doctrine of the Bible. To judge, however, without bias, a supposition or two must be made.

Suppose, first, that a stranger to our controversies were to state what, in his judgment, is implied in these texts. We can anticipate his exposition. He would give us their first and obvious meaning, of infant baptism or sprinkling he would say nothing; the very idea, it is more than probable, would never occur to him. Make the experiment another way. Suppose adult baptism universally practised, infant sprinkling *unknown*, and these texts, for the first time, urged to prove it our duty to alter our worship, and adopt infant sprinkling. It is easy to conceive what would happen; instantly and unanimously it would be said—"These texts speak nothing of infant sprinkling; all of them treat of other subjects: the practice proposed might be inferred from Ezra's genealogies, or from the chambers in Ezekiel's temple, as soon as from these texts". The whole evidence would be treated with scorn and contempt, and the proposal universally rejected.

If it be your judgment that such would be the result in the case supposed, it is of course your judgment that infant sprinkling cannot naturally be inferred from any text in the New Testament. But let us suppose that the inquirer imagines, that from these texts inferences may be drawn favourable to the cause of Pædo-baptism. What is to be done? The apostolical practice, I answer, will effectually determine the correctness or incorrectness of the alleged or imagined inferences. The practice of the Apostles in this matter shall be minutely examined; and if it shall be found, as it certainly will, that there is no evidence that they either baptized infants, or instructed men to baptize them, we must yield to the determination of fact. Inferences to the contrary must be fallacious, whether I shall be able to expose the fallacy or not.

III. A third kind of inference in support of Pædo-baptism is drawn from *institutions already appointed, but now discontinued by Divine authority.* Inferences of this kind are altogether illogical. Positive evangelical institutions cannot be inferred from legal institutions now abrogated.

The truth of this assertion may be evinced in many ways.

1. It has been shown that *Christ alone is Lord of Gospel institutions.* Be pleased to observe that it is in the exercise of sovereignty that he appoints these institutions. Now, the effects of the exercise of infinite sovereignty we cannot possibly anticipate. Sovereignty, it is true, is always exercised according to the attributes of Divinity. As to us, however, since we do not possess these attributes, it is impossible to discover the determining causes. For example, amongst the tribes of Israel, could we possibly anticipate the tribe to be elected for the priesthood? Facts speak the same language. There were four distinct branches of the Old Dispensation. On comparison, we shall find that no two of these branches have the same positive institutions. For instance, in the two first branches (under Adam and Noah), neither parents nor children were circumcised. It was otherwise in the third and fourth (under Abraham and Moses). These things are sufficient proof that positive evangelical institutions cannot be inferred from legal institutions now abrogated. Were I to judge of the subjects of baptism from inference, I would infer

that they were not the same as the subjects of circumcision. My reason for so inferring, is the manifold differences by which the different branches of the Old Dispensation had been distinguished one from another. My inference is justified by the fact. The subjects of circumcision and baptism are not the same. But had I not been previously acquainted with this fact, I could with certainty have inferred nothing either on the one side or the other.

2. *Positive evangelical institutions cannot be inferred from legal institutions, now abrogated, without violating the simplicity of the Gospel.* We are commanded to keep the ordinances as the Apostles delivered them to us. We are commanded to stand fast, and hold the traditions which they have taught us. Were we to infer positive institutions from other positive institutions, such institutions might be multiplied without end. On the same principle that the Pædo-baptist infers infant-sprinkling from circumcision, he might infer the pontiff, the popish jubilee, and the mass, from the high-priest, jubilee, and sacrifices of the Israelites. The inclination to Judaize has infected different societies in different degrees. Its effects on Papists, Episcopalians, and others, are sufficiently known. But it is evident that if the principle on which baptism is inferred from circumcision be acted on at all, no limits can be set to the procedure: there is an end of the simplicity of the Gospel Dispensation.

3. *I cannot observe institutions, inferred from other institutions, with full satisfaction of mind.* I am perplexed with a number of unanswerable questions. Take the following as a specimen. From which of the abrogated institutions am I to draw inferences?

From all, from some, or from one only? How many institutions am I to infer from each? How am I to modify my inferred institutions? Is every man to infer institutions for himself; or is one man, as in the Papacy, or many, as in Prelacy, to draw the inferences? No answer can be given to these questions, and yet answers are essential to satisfaction in duty. For anything I know, I may have too many inferences, or too few, or such as I should not have. Such a doubtful state of mind is expressly excluded from worship: Rom. xiv. 5—23.

In inquiring whether New Testament institutions may be inferred from those of the Old Testament, it must never be forgotten, that the positive institutions of the Old Dispensation are abrogated. Abrogated institutions have no existence; every inference deduced from them is illusory. Of nothing, I repeat the logical aphorism, men can make nothing; from nothing, nothing can be inferred.

This is especially the case in the matter before us. The repeal of the law of circumcision is specially recorded. Were I to reason on inference, it is from the repeal, and not from the institution, that I would reason; and my inference would be this, that, excepting with the antitype, that is, personal holiness, I am no way concerned with the law of circumcision. From it I can learn nothing of the character of the institutions of the New Dispensation.

4. *The observance of institutions founded on inference is, in effect, prohibited.* We do not expect that every error in doctrine, government, discipline, and worship, is in the Scriptures to be particularly

marked and refuted. Whatever is inconsistent with revelation is wrong. As to positive ordinances, and particularly Baptism, we have all our instructions in the Scriptures. There is no room for additions. The Apostles have taught us to observe all things whatsoever Christ has commanded us. There is no room for reduction or alteration. The same authority requires us to observe all the ordinances as they were delivered; 1 Cor. xi. 2. The consequence of disobedience is separation: 2 Thess. iii. 6. As these things are true of positive institutions in general, so are they true of Baptism in particular. Respecting this institution our instructions are complete. Thus we have seen that institutions cannot be observed on inference, either from the procedure of professing Christians, from the Scriptures usually alleged, or from the abrogated rites of the Old Dispensation.

I shall now conclude this lecture with a few general remarks. First, We have no instructions, either by precept or example, to found positive ordinances on inference. My second remark respects the unhappy consequences of tampering with revelation.

Inferential reasoning on the point in question, like every other tradition of man, makes void the commandments of God. I assume two facts, known already, it is probable, to the inquirer, and which shall afterwards be proved by incontestable evidence. The first is, that every man after believing is, by the Scriptures, obliged to be baptized. The second is, that infant sprinkling is nowhere enjoined in the Scriptures. Mark, now, the effect of inference. Men do what is virtually forbidden, and neglect what is positively required. Except such as were not sprinkled in infancy, no adult persons are baptized by the Pædo-baptists. Infant sprinkling, on the contrary, engrosses the attention of their churches. The work enjoined by our heavenly Master has, in a great measure, been omitted, whilst his professed servants have been wasting their time in operations which he never required.

Take another example of the unhappy consequences of founding institutions on inference, namely, the lamentable divisions and sub-divisions of professing Christians. One man thinks he sees the inference, and acts on the imagination; another cannot see the inference, and rejects the practice which grows out of it. Suppose that both these men seriously believe and practise their principles—division is inevitable. There is one way, and but one, of uniting Christians, and that is, for all of us to act on revelation as we find it. The fact accords with these statements:—men have never agreed (at least since inquiry has been excited) either in the practice of infant sprinkling, or in the inferences on which it is founded. The less learned inquirer may need to be informed that, even though Pædo-baptists agree in the practice of infant sprinkling, they are at variance amongst themselves respecting the inferences on which they found it.

In the end of the last century a work was published on infant sprinkling. The author collects all the inferences in its favour, and proves by quotations, that every one of these inferences has been rejected as illegitimate by men of distinction who adhered to the practice. Suppose, now, what has often happened, that all these inferences should appear to the inquirer to be as groundless as each of them has appeared to one or other of the abettors of sprinkling. What is the consequence? Division follows, of course. Expedients may conceal the evil, but they cannot cure it; and the more extensively this pernicious principle is acted upon, the more are divisions multiplied, extended, and imbittered. What was said before, we must repeat in this place—There is one way, and but one, of uniting Christians, and that is by receiving the Christian institutions, not from inference, but from the doctrine or example of Scripture.

LECTURE VII.

PRESUMPTIONS AGAINST INFANT BAPTISM.

The abettors of Infant Baptism have endeavoured to vindicate their practice by a kind of cumulative or presumptive evidence. They introduce their reasoning as follows. "Suppose, for the sake of argument, that not one of our proofs, taken by itself, should appear satisfactory, yet all of them taken together warrant our practice. Recollect the extent and antiquity of the practice, the circumcision of infants, the prophecies respecting children in the Old Testament, and all the texts in the New respecting households, the holiness and blessings of infants, and the rest. Take these things together, and the lawfulness, if not the necessity, of our practice is sufficiently vindicated."

To this mode of reasoning it were sufficient to reply, that cumulative evidence is of force, then, and then only, when all the particulars in the assemblage contribute to strengthen the cause; but where each particular is inefficient, the whole is inefficient. The presumption is not greater from the whole than it is from any of the parts. An accumulation of ciphers amounts to nothing. The object, however, of a conscientious inquirer is, not the refutation of others, but the satisfaction of his own mind. We must, therefore, examine the presumptions against infant baptism, that the presumptions for and against it may be thrown into opposite scales, and the judgment of the inquirer may be determined by that which preponderates.

To some of the presumptions against infant baptism it has been objected, "that the Scriptures on which they are founded concern adults only, that they do not concern infants, and that although certain qualifications are required in the baptism of adults, it does not follow that like qualifications are required to the baptism of infants: even as it cannot be said that infants are interdicted from eating by the apostolic injunction in 2 Thess. iii. 10."

It is answered, 1. In the text quoted, infants are obviously excepted; it is those who are able, but unwilling to work, that are mentioned. But although the words had run thus, as they do not, "If any work not, neither should he eat", still the nourishment of infants would not have been prohibited. The reason is plain; the support of infants is elsewhere required; and this explicit requisition exempts them from the general rule. 2. As to the matter of the objection,—Recollect that infants are in no part of Scripture excepted from the usual requisites for baptism, and that infant baptism is nowhere enjoined. Were it otherwise, infants must be baptized, notwithstanding their want of qualifications, &c., but as the fact stands, the want of the requisite qualifications bars their baptism.

Take a parallel case for illustration:—The qualifications for the Lord's Supper refer to adults only; yet in this country, professing Christians, Pædo-baptists not excepted, hold that they are such as must exclude infants from communion. All say that the worthy communicant must be able to discern the Lord's body, for the Scriptures require such discernment: on the same grounds, we say that the baptized must possess the scriptural qualifications. Infants are excluded from both ordinances on the same ground. The example carries the matter farther; it bars the argument from inference. It is known that the pleas for infant communion are the same with the pleas for infant baptism. All of them, however, are repelled by the consideration of the requisites for partaking of the Supper. A conscientious regard to truth requires similar procedure in similar circumstances. The qualifications necessary to the baptized prevent us from observing infant baptism on inference. I shall only add, that some of the presumptions are founded on facts essential to baptism. No remembrance of Christ; no partaking of the Supper. No reception of the truth; no baptism. Add to this consideration the want of exception in favour of infants, and the want of command respecting the baptism of infants, and the objection is still farther removed; the presumptions being strengthened that infants are not the scriptural subjects of that ordinance.

I. The first presumption against infant sprinkling arises from THE SILENCE OF THE SCRIPTURES ON THE SUBJECT. The silence of the Scriptures on the sprinkling or baptism of infants, is known to all who have read the Bible. We speak not at present of inferences, but of expressions. On this topic not a single word occurs either in the Old

Testament or in the New. This fact is universally acknowledged; it cannot be denied. From this fact arise various presumptions unfavourable to the popular practice. Infant baptism is never mentioned in Scripture. None of the parties interested have received any instructions concerning it. The parties concerned are infants, parents, children, teachers, and the churches. Let us consider them in their order.

1. *The infants to be sprinkled are not specified.* We are nowhere told what infants are, and what infants are not, to be sprinkled. Instructions are necessary to all appointed worship; but, in the present case, they are peculiarly necessary. Many questions arise on the right to sprinkling, whether the right be supposed to be lodged in the infants or in the parents. If the right be lodged in the infants, the question will be, Ought all infants to be sprinkled? or some only? If all ought to be sprinkled, why are not missionaries employed to gain the consent of parents, and sprinkle infants everywhere, at home and abroad? If some only are to be sprinkled; if grace be required, how is it to be ascertained in infants? How are we to distinguish the gracious infants from the graceless babes? Suppose the right invested in the parents; the question, then, will be, who are to be sponsors? The parents exclusively? or others? If others, what others? From what parents is the right derived? The immediate or the remote? The father, or the mother, or both? The abettors of infant baptism are divided on these questions. The practice differs in different communions. But be the practice what it may, a warrant is required, and

cannot be produced. On all these questions the silence of the Scriptures is profound. Had God required the sprinkling of infants, the infants to be sprinkled would certainly have been specified.

2. *Parents are deeply interested, but never directed in this imaginary duty.* They are nowhere instructed to teach their children to improve their baptism; and, what ought to be particularly noticed, parents are nowhere required to have their children baptized. The instructions to parents are many and minute; they are repeatedly commanded to train up their children in the nurture and admonition of the Lord, and repeatedly instructed in the import of this nurture and admonition. But is it not unaccountably strange, that one of the chief parental duties should never once be hinted at in Scripture? If infant sprinkling be a duty, it is a most momentous duty; it would be amongst the first and greatest duties which parents owe to their children. Although nothing had been revealed of other parental duties, we should have expected, from its importance, that this would have been fully explained, and repeatedly inculcated; it is evident, however, that the fact accords not with this expectation. Infant baptism is no parental duty; it is one of the corruptions of Christianity, and its foundation, like the foundation of Popery, is sapped by the silence of Scripture.

3. *Children and youth are interested, but they are never directed to improve their infant baptism or sprinkling.* The instructions given to believers in general may easily be applied to the young; and, no doubt, the general instructions respecting baptism are as applicable to them as to others. In

other things, however, the Holy Spirit has not left them to general admonitions, he has favoured them with special instructions. He has taught them to know the Scriptures, to obey their parents, to be sober-minded, to be humble, to be submissive. He has enforced these duties by various motives; such as a regard to rectitude, to their own best interests, and the like. But of their baptism in infancy he speaks not a word; they are neither taught to improve it for duty, motive, or comfort; and they are never, directly or indirectly, so much as reminded of the fact. For this significant silence there must be a cause; and the most natural cause is, that infant baptism was unknown to the apostles.

There are two other parties concerned. *The evangelists*, I mean, and *the churches;* but I need not enlarge on these. The remarks already made are so certainly and so easily applicable, that to mention them should be sufficient. The apostles, particularly Paul, had occasion, repeatedly, to address both the evangelists and the churches. The former are fully instructed in all that they had to teach; the latter are instructed as to every part of their faith and practice; but neither the one nor the other receives a single hint on the sprinkling or baptizing of infants. Luke entitles his second work, The Acts, or the actings, of the Apostles: if the apostles baptized infants, and their historian has not recorded the fact, how are we to reconcile the omission with his character as a faithful historian? He professes to record the practice of the apostles; but if they sprinkled or baptized infants, he has not verified his profession; a part of their practice, most common and interesting, is not once either exemplified or mentioned. His silence on this head becomes the more remarkable, as he is particular in recording the concerns of children, when they occurred. Take an example, Acts xxi. 5. Relating the events at Tyre, in Paul's journey towards Jerusalem, he tells us that the apostle was conducted to the shore by the disciples, both men and women, and takes particular notice of their children. Compare with this account of the children the history of Philip's baptizing at Samaria, Acts viii. 12. He tells us that men were baptized, and that women were baptized, but there is no mention of children. Permit me to ask, why children are so carefully noticed in the one case, and omitted in the other? The answer is obvious: the parents with their children accompanied Paul; but Philip baptized no infants. On the supposition that it was the usual practice of the apostles to baptize infants, it is impossible to reconcile the silence of Luke either with accuracy or fidelity. To judge here as we ought, however, two things should be observed:—1. That Luke is writing under the direction of the Holy Ghost; 2. That the design of his history is, by the practice of the apostles, to direct the worship of all the churches to the end of the world. The history accords with the fact, and by both the churches are taught, in imitation of the apostles, to restrict baptism to professing believers.

II. A second presumption against infant sprinkling arises from WHAT THE SCRIPTURES DO TEACH OF BAPTISM. They treat of it frequently, fully, and in a great variety of forms. It is taught in doctrines, in precepts, in examples, and in inferences. But wherever, or in what form soever, the subject occurs, it is restricted exclusively to adults. This is known to all who are acquainted with the Bible. What do we learn from this? If adult baptism be inculcated frequently,—if infant baptism be never hinted at, the presumption is plain:—in adult baptism we are very deeply interested; but with infant baptism we have nothing to do. Judge from a similar case. Respecting the qualifications and duties of elders, we have full information: but the Scriptures speak nothing of popes or of prelates. Accordingly, we reject popery and prelacy, and receive the elders of the Scriptures. In reason and consistency we are bound, in the matter of Baptism, to form a similar judgment, and to pursue a similar practice. Infant sprinkling, like popery, is nowhere enjoined in the Scriptures, and like it, must of course be rejected. Adult baptism is frequently and strongly pressed on our consciences, and must, like the scriptural eldership, be received and obeyed. The presumption is strengthened by comparing the Scripture doctrine of baptism with the actual state of the Church.

Suppose Pædo-baptism to be the truth, the number of adults will bear no proportion to the number of infants to be baptized. The total amount of the adults could not exceed the number of converts from the superstitions of Jews, Mahommedans, and Heathens. The number of infants would be incalculably greater, particularly in the Millennium. During this period, the Jews, and the fulness of the Gentiles, being converted, almost none, excepting infants, remain to be baptized.

Observe, then, the Church, through the extent of her history, and the infants are by far the most numerous class; the adults to be baptized are comparatively few. From the wisdom and care of their Ruler, I expect revelation to be adapted to the exigencies of his people. I expect instructions on adult baptism, because adults are to be baptized; but I expect more full, more particular instructions on Pædo-baptism, because, on the supposition of its being a Christian ordinance, infants will form the majority of those to whom it is administered. Compare these reasonable expectations with the fact, and it at once appears that the Scripture doctrine of baptism is not adapted to the baptism of infants. On adult baptism I have the most ample information; but if pædo-baptism be our duty, the Scriptures afford me no information on the subject. In no part of them can I find any provision made for the supply of this want. The inference is clear: this want or defect is merely imaginary; revelation is not adapted to pædo-baptism. Infant baptism is a corruption of Christianity; it is not regulated by the Scriptures, and must therefore be rejected by the disciples of Christ. The baptism of believers ought exclusively to be practised, and so it undoubtedly will be in the Millennium. All the pleas for infant baptism are cut off. The more obscure passages must be explained by the passages that are more clear. Casual references must be explained by the passages which treat more fully of the subject. Whatever is said of circumcision, households, the blessings and holiness of children, and the like, must be explained by the commission and the Acts of the Apostles. The practice of infant baptism is not sanctioned by the commission and Acts of the Apostles; and, consequently, by nothing in the Scriptures. What is the consequence? It cannot be practised in faith, for faith cometh by the word of God. It cannot be administered or received in the name of Christ; for to baptize in the name of Christ is, amongst other things, to baptize by his commission.

Infant sprinkling, like every other unscriptural practice, must be rejected as will-worship: "Why, as though living in the world,* are ye subject to ordinances . . . after the commandments and doctrines of men?" Col. ii. 20, 22.

---

* Here the *world* evidently means the Jewish dispensation, the worldly kingdom established in Israel.—J. H.

LECTURE VIII.

FARTHER PRESUMPTIONS AGAINST INFANT BAPTISM.

III. A third presumption against infant baptism arises out of THE NECESSITY OF BEING SATISFIED THAT IT IS THE WILL OF GOD.

Satisfaction as to our duty, in every part of the service of God, is frequently required in the Scriptures. "And whatsoever ye do in word or deed, do all in the name of the Lord Jesus": Col. iii. 17. "Let every man be fully persuaded in his own mind": "Whatsoever is not of faith is sin": Romans xiv. 5, 23. These rules must be applied to Baptism as well as to other things, especially as the same injunction is implied, if not expressed, in the common formula of administration.

Satisfaction as to our duty is thus required, but how is it to be found? For infant baptism there is neither doctrine, nor precept, nor example, nor evident inference. All the evidence offered is some unproved inferences drawn from irrelevant premises by a circuitous process of ratiocination. Whether these inferences have in any instance proved satisfactory, each individual must judge. They furnish a pretext, indeed, for such as desire a pretext, but they are ill calculated for giving satisfaction to the conscientious worshipper.

IV. A fourth presumption against infant baptism arises from THE QUALIFICATIONS REQUIRED IN THE BAPTIZED. The first qualification requisite in baptism is *knowledge*, of which infants are incapable. The necessity of knowledge to baptism is implied in every baptismal qualification. This necessity is expressly taught in Matt. xxviii. 19, 20, " Go ye therefore and teach all nations, baptizing them in the name of the Father, and of the Son, and of the Holy Ghost: teaching them to observe all things whatsoever I have commanded you". In these few words, the necessity of knowledge to baptism is mentioned in three different ways. 1. The apostles are commanded to teach the nations. 2. They are commanded to baptize the disciples in the name of the Trinity; that is, into the belief of the things which they had been taught respecting the Trinity,—into the faith of the Father, Son, and Holy Spirit. 3. They are commanded to teach the baptized after their baptism, as they had taught them before it: "Teaching them to observe all things whatsoever I have commanded you".

Objections have been made to this testimony. The word "teach" in the beginning of the verses, might, say the objectors, be rendered "disciple", or, make disciples of the nations. But the objection is irrelevant,—the translation is sufficiently correct; and though the word were altered, the meaning would remain. To disciple, implies teaching.* Further, what Matthew calls

---

* The argument is strengthened, not weakened, by rendering the word in the first clause, *disciple*, or make

teach, or disciple, Mark renders "*preach* the gospel to every creature". To teach them, therefore, is to preach to them the gospel. What is baptizing into the Trinity, but baptizing into what we are taught concerning the Trinity? As to the "teaching" in the second clause, the translation cannot be altered.

I need not say that infants are incapable of being taught, or of being baptized into the name or faith of the Trinity. In these words there is no exception of infants. This has indeed been suggested, but the suggestion refutes itself. It is obvious, from the commission, that the subjects of baptism must first be taught, or made disciples. Unless, then, we find in some part of Scripture an exception in regard to infants, they must be excluded from baptism. They want the requisite qualification of knowledge.

Faith, which infants do not possess, is a second qualification requisite to baptism, of which infants are incapable. That faith is necessary to baptism appears from many scriptures. I quote a few as examples. "He that believeth and is baptized shall be saved": Mark xvi. 16. "And Philip said, If thou believest with all thine heart, thou mayest" (be baptized): Acts viii. 37. "Buried with him in baptism, wherein also ye are risen with him through the faith of the operation of God": Col. ii. 12. These, and other scriptures, prove that faith is necessary to baptism.

---

disciples; they are first to be instructed, and then baptized. Thus we read (John iv. 1,) that the Pharisees had heard that Jesus *made and baptized* more disciples than John.— J. H.

I must not take leave of this particular, without reminding the inquirer of two things: 1. That every objection known to the writer, has been anticipated in this, or some preceding lecture; 2. That self-examination and discerning the Lord's body are not more essential to the observance of the Lord's supper, than faith is to baptism. From Mark I learn, that baptism without faith is of no avail. From Luke I learn, that if the Ethiopian had not believed with all his heart, he could not have been baptized. From Paul I learn that the Colossians rose with Christ in baptism, only through the faith of the operation of God, who hath raised Christ from the dead. This last testimony is particularly to be considered, because it extends to all to whom the epistle is directed. Its doctrine is that faith is essential to baptism, and is not restricted to any particular class of the baptized. The conclusion is irresistible. Infants cannot be baptized, because they cannot believe, or, what is practically the same thing, they cannot give evidence of their faith.

Repentance is a third qualification requisite in baptism, of which infants are incapable. The connection between repentance and baptism is asserted or implied in many Scriptures. "I indeed," says John, "baptize you with water unto repentance": Matt. iii. 11. "Now when they heard this, they were pricked in their heart, and said unto Peter and to the rest of the apostles, Men and brethren, what shall we do? Then Peter said unto them, Repent and be baptized every one of you in the name of Jesus Christ for the remission of sins, and ye shall receive the gift of the Holy Ghost": Acts ii. 37, 38. "And now why tarriest thou? arise, and be baptized, and wash away thy sins, calling on the name of the Lord": Acts xxii. 16. In this manner the Scriptures teach us the connection between repentance and baptism. In the passages quoted, there is no exception of infants from the general rule. Repentance is necessary to baptism; and children cannot be baptized, because they cannot repent.

Holiness is the fourth qualification requisite to baptism. The necessity of holiness to the baptized is often intimated. "Jesus answered (Nicodemus), Verily, verily, I say unto thee, Except a man be born of water and of the Spirit, he cannot enter into the kingdom of God": John iii. 5. "According to his mercy he saved us, by the washing of regeneration and renewing of the Holy Ghost": Titus iii. 5. Infants are capable of holiness, (Jer. i. 5); but all infants are not holy; and no infant can give the evidence of holiness required in the Scriptures.

Putting on Christ is a fifth qualification requisite to baptism. "For as many of you as have been baptized into Christ have put on Christ": Gal. iii. 27. The figure is taken from putting on clothes: it implies an action on the part of the person baptized, of which infants are incapable. In baptism the believer professes his faith in Christ. The process here is short, and the conclusion certain. Infants cannot put on Christ, and consequently cannot be baptized. Consider what is implied in putting on Christ, and this will appear still more evident. By Christ, we are to understand the doctrine concerning Christ. 1 Cor. ii. 2,

"For I determined not to know any thing among you, save Jesus Christ, and him crucified",—not the philosophy of the Greeks; not the ceremonies of the Jews; but what is written concerning the person, character, offices, and work of Christ. To preach Christ, then, is to preach the truth concerning him. And what is it "to put on Christ", but to understand, believe, apply, and practise that truth? The apostle frequently uses the words in this sense. "Let us walk honestly, as in the day; not in rioting and drunkenness, not in chambering and wantonness, not in strife and envying. But put ye on the Lord Jesus Christ, and make not provision for the flesh, to fulfil the lusts thereof": Rom. xiii. 13, 14. "But now ye also put off all these; anger, wrath, malice, blasphemy, filthy communication out of your mouth. Lie not one to another, seeing that ye have put off the old man with his deeds; and have put on the new man, which is renewed in knowledge, after the image of him that created him": Col. iii. 8—10. We have, in our own language, expressions of the same kind. We speak of "laying aside bad habits, and acquiring good habits". The general meaning of the passages quoted is similar. To put off the old man and put on the new, is the purpose and practice of reformation; putting on Christ, is the purpose and practice of obeying the Gospel. Observe, next, the comprehensive and unlimited form of the apostle's assertion. "For as many of you as have been baptized into Christ, have put on Christ": Gal. iii. 27. He does not mean that some of the Galatian Christians were baptized and some not. All the members of the churches of

Galatia were baptized. He does not merely mean that the baptized were all bound in duty to reformation : the fact is asserted,—as many of them as were baptized had put on Christ. He means that reformation was essential to baptism, and that every individual baptized either was, or appeared to be, reformed ; there was no exception of Jew or Greek, of learned or unlearned, of young or old. The presumption that infants cannot be baptized, is strengthened, because they are incapable of moral agency, and of the actions described and required by the apostle.

A sixth qualification requisite to baptism, which cannot be found in infants, is *the answer of a good conscience.* " The like figure whereunto even baptism doth also now save us (not the putting away of the filth of the flesh, but the answer of a good conscience toward God), by the resurrection of Jesus Christ " : 1 Peter iii. 21. Here the apostle represents believers as being, in figure, saved by baptism; but in order to guard them against imagining that salvation was necessarily connected with the observance of the ordinance, he says, "not the putting away the filth of the flesh ", but the answer of a good conscience, &c. In baptism, the believer professes his faith in Christ for the remission of his sins, and that by his resurrection he is begotten to a lively hope of salvation : 1 Pet. i. 3. " It is God that justifieth, who is he that condemneth? It is Christ that died ; yea rather, that is risen again " : Rom. viii. 33, 34. Thus he has the answer of a good conscience ; his heart no more condemns him. This is the beginning of the believer's confidence, which he is commanded to hold steadfast to the end: Heb. iii. 14.

Now, every one must see the consequence; infants cannot be baptized, because they cannot have the answer of a good conscience. To this consequence an objection has been made. Paul says, in Rom. ii. 28, 29, "He is not a Jew which is one outwardly; neither is that circumcision which is outward in the flesh: but he is a Jew which is one inwardly; and circumcision is that of the heart, in the spirit, and not in the letter; whose praise is not of men, but of God". And it has been asked, will any one hence argue that the Jewish infants, for want of this, were not to be admitted into covenant with God by circumcision? To this question I answer, 1. Paul is speaking of circumcision, and Peter of baptism. These ordinances must be proved to be similar, before relevant conclusions can be drawn from the one to the other. 2. It is true that circumcision, without regeneration, could not save the Jew, and that baptism, if the conscience be not good, will not save the baptized. 3. Baptism requires a profession of faith in all its subjects, which circumcision did not.

I have now given six examples of qualifications required in baptism, of all which infants are incapable. These are knowledge, faith, repentance, holiness, putting on Christ, and the answer of a good conscience. It has been proved that each of these stands connected with baptism, in the same way that self-examination and discerning the Lord's body stand connected with The Supper. It has been shown that the objections to infants observing both ordinances are similar, and similarly answered; and, in particular, that infants are not excepted from the general rules. The presumption, then, is very strong: if the want of qualifications represented in Scripture as essential to the observance of the ordinance should exclude infants from the Lord's supper, must not the want of similar qualifications exclude them from baptism? It is not easy to see that anything can be opposed to these remarks, without reflecting on the wisdom, or care, or authority of him who hath given us the Scriptures as the rule of our worship.

V. A fifth presumption against infant sprinkling arises from THE DUTIES CONNECTED WITH BAPTISM. For our present purpose, it will not be necessary to enumerate these duties, it is sufficient to give examples of them. If it prove true that there are duties required in baptism which infants cannot perform, it will follow that infants cannot be baptized. The following examples will satisfy the inquirer that there are duties of this description.

1. I mention as my first example *a profession of the faith*. The necessity of professing the faith is often taught in the Scriptures. "Whosoever therefore shall confess me before men, him will I confess also before my Father which is in heaven. But whosoever shall deny me before men, him will I also deny before my Father which is in heaven": Matt. x. 32. "If thou shalt confess with thy mouth the Lord Jesus, and shalt believe in thine heart that God hath raised him from the dead, thou shalt be saved. For with the heart man believeth unto righteousness, and with the mouth confession is

made unto salvation": Rom. x. 9.* The connection between confessing the faith and baptism, appears likewise in many ways:—(1.) From the circumstances in which the apostles propagated the gospel. They preached to the Jews and heathen; such of their hearers as believed professed their faith and were baptized. Thus, at Corinth, Paul preached, and many of the Corinthians hearing, believed and were baptized. (2.) The connection between professing the faith and baptism is implied in the commission to the apostles, and in similar Scriptures. The administrator could only learn from their profession of faith who they were who believed. The account which we have of the Ethiopian's baptism confirms all that has been said.

2. I take my next example from the concomitant duties—*the duties required of the baptized at the time of their immersion.* In the Supper, more is required than the mere corporeal acts of eating bread and drinking wine. We must remember Christ: without this worship of the mind the bodily service is useless. The case is similar in baptism. We are baptized for the remission of sins, into the death of Christ, into Christ, into the name of the Father, Son, and Holy Spirit. Our

---

* Here the apostle represents two things as being essential to salvation, believing with the heart, and confessing with the mouth. Now, baptism is the appointed mode of confession, and hence we read, "He that believeth and is baptized shall be saved". Believers, from not knowing their Master's will, may not observe the ordinance, and others may be baptized on a false profession of faith; but we see the importance of baptism from its being the only ordinance, the observance of which Christ in the commission has connected with salvation. —J. H.

minds must go into the truth respecting these things, as our bodies go into the water. The mere corporeal operation is as useless here as in the Supper. "God is a spirit, and they that worship him must worship him in spirit and in truth." "Bodily exercise profiteth little": 1 Tim. iv. 8. Peter expressly applies these things to baptism, 1 Peter iii. 21; Acts xxii. 16. But it is not necessary to quote particular Scriptures: the very design of baptism implies that the mind must be exercised about what the ordinance represents.

3. I take my next example from *the duties consequent upon baptism.* I name but two, church association, and the practice of the truth. (1.) In ordinary cases, it is the duty of the baptized, without exception, *to form themselves into churches,* or *to unite themselves with churches* already formed. "Teaching them to observe all things whatsoever I have commanded you": Matt. xxviii. 19. Amongst the things commanded by Christ, church association holds a prominent place. And, it ought to be observed, that there is to be no unnecessary interval. As soon as a man is taught, he ought to believe; as soon as he believes, he ought to be baptized; as soon as he is baptized, he ought to join the church. Acts ii. explains the commission. Verses 41, 42: "Then they that gladly received the word were baptized; and the same day there were added unto them about three thousand souls. And they continued stedfastly in the apostles' doctrine and fellowship, and in breaking of bread, and in prayers". The three thousand were baptized, and added to the church on the same day, *i. e.,* without

delay. "For by one Spirit are we all baptized into one body, whether we be Jews or Gentiles, whether we be bond or free; and have been all made to drink into one Spirit": 1 Cor. xii. 13. All are baptized into one body, and the apostle is reasoning on the principle that the church of Corinth represented that one body in Corinth. Our obligation to join a particular church is thus implied in our baptism. Agreeably to these Scriptures, I find a church in Jerusalem, in Corinth, and in other cities; but I find neither precept nor example for separating baptism from the supper. Baptism is an ordinance of initiation. Amongst other things, it is designed to signify that we profess ourselves Christians, and that others ought to treat us accordingly. Without baptism we cannot, consistently with the rules of Scripture, be admitted to church fellowship; but being baptized, if there be no obstructions, we ought not to be kept from church communion, either by ourselves or others. The case of the Ethiopian is, from its nature, extraordinary.

Pædo-baptists and sprinklers have been greatly puzzled as to the position of baptized infants in the Church. Some of the infant-baptizers have admitted them to the Supper. Infant-sprinklers—from the establishment of the doctrine of transubstantiation—have excluded them from the Supper, but received them to a kind of equivocal church membership.

(2.) *The practice of the truth* was my other example of duties consequent on baptism. This example comprehends learning and practising whatever Christ has commanded. Of these things infants are incapable.

To conclude this particular, let us recollect, that, without exception of young or old, *duties which infants cannot perform are required in the baptized. By every class of these duties, whether before, at, or after the ordinance, infants must be excluded from baptism.*

LECTURE IX.

FURTHER PRESUMPTIONS AGAINST INFANT BAPTISM.

VI. Another presumption against infant baptism, arises from THE SCRIPTURES REJECTING THE PRINCIPLES ON WHICH IT RESTS.

The right of the infant to baptism is derived from different sources by Pædo-baptists. Some found it on the commission given by our Lord to his disciples, alleging that men are to be made disciples by means of baptism. The fallacy of this appears by comparing the commission as recorded by Matthew, Mark, and Luke. Disciples or believers—for the terms are synonymous—can only be made by instruction, and consequently, our right to baptism is founded on our faith; in other words, upon our knowledge of the truth as it is in Jesus.

Others found the infant's right to baptism upon an imaginary grace supposed to be common to all men. But this principle is disproved by the arguments which disprove Arminianism. The most popular opinion is, that the right to baptism runs in the blood, the title being derived from the parents or ancestors. Infants descended more immediately or more remotely from believers are considered as infants of a privileged order. Some maintain that all infants ought to be baptized or sprinkled, because of our common descent from believing Noah. Some refer the right to the faith of the immediate father or mother; others take a different view. But the very basis of the popular practice is the supposition that the souls of infants derive benefit or injury from their carnal descent. The Scriptures reject this principle; and if this assertion be proved, so far as this principle is concerned, infant baptism must fall with its foundation. But I must open the way for my proof by a few preliminary remarks.

1. The chain of reasoning here will be short and strong; but, however strong, I would never have opposed it to the slightest intimation of fact. Had God taught us to baptize infants, either by precept, by example, or in any other way, it would have been my duty to subject all my reasoning to revelation. But if I am told, without any other intimation of the will of God, that the child by its descent from a believing parent is entitled to spiritual privileges, because the Israelites, by their descent from Abraham, were entitled to typical privileges, I am obliged to examine this principle; and if it appear that till Christ came, *descent*, by Divine appointment, gave the descendant from Abraham a right to circumcision, but that *descent*, by the same authority, now confers no spiritual privilege, the principle must be rejected, and along with it the consequent practice.

2. We by no means assert that children may not be profited or hurt by means of their parents. A child may inherit a constitution healthy or diseased; he may be born to a great estate, or to personal

PRESUMPTIONS AGAINST INFANT BAPTISM. 95

poverty; he may be trained to every species of wickedness, or brought up in the nurture and admonition of the Lord. The effects of education, good or bad, are universally allowed to be very great. We assert, only, that the soul of a child is not immediately affected by carnal descent.*

3. We do not suppose that infant grace would prove infant baptism, any more than it would prove infant communion. Though grace were possessed, yet the possessor could not be admitted either to baptism or the Lord's-supper, until he professed his faith, and could exercise grace; so much at least as to answer the design of these ordinances. It is a very common, though a very palpable mistake, to confound grace—and what is still more absurd, the mere possibility of having grace—with the exercise and profession of it. Though grace did run in the blood, infants, or even children, could not be admitted either to baptism or the Supper until they professed their faith, and gave evidence of understanding these acts of worship. Without understanding, the ordinances would not be spiritual services, and therefore could not be acceptable to God.

4. It is not to be expected that the Scriptures should specify and refute every particular error. Errors are countless. It is sufficient that the truth be stated; whatever opposes truth is error. The duty of restricting baptism to those who are capable of professing their faith, is fully and plainly revealed. Infant baptism, if not specially enjoined, is opposed to truth, and must be discontinued.

5. It is, however, not a little remarkable, that the kindness of the prescient Spirit of our heavenly

---

* We are not now speaking of original sin.

Father has put us on our guard here by more than ordinary instruction. He has not only, by stating the truth, furnished us with the means of detecting error, but particularly has taught us to reject it, by rejecting the principle on which it rests.

Let us take some examples of the doctrine of Scripture on the subject of carnal descent. "But when he (John the Baptist) saw many of the Pharisees and Sadducees come to his baptism, he said unto them, O generation of vipers, who hath warned you to flee from the wrath to come? Bring forth therefore fruits meet for repentance; and think not to say within yourselves, We have Abraham to our father: for I say unto you, that God is able of these stones to raise up children unto Abraham. And now also the axe is laid unto the root of the trees: therefore every tree which bringeth not forth good fruit is hewn down, and cast into the fire. I indeed baptize you with water unto repentance: but he that cometh after me is mightier than I, whose shoes I am not worthy to bear: he shall baptize you with the Holy Ghost and with fire: whose fan is in his hand, and he will throughly purge his floor, and gather his wheat into the garner; but he will burn up the chaff with unquenchable fire": Mat. iii. 7—12.

In this passage, we may observe the following things:—(1.) According to the Sinai covenant, a male descendant from Abraham, when circumcised, became a member of the typical community; grace was not necessary. The Pharisees and Sadducees, though a generation of vipers, were legitimate members of that community. John tells them that the antitype differed from the type; that personal religion, "fruits meet for repentance", were requisite in the subjects of the kingdom of heaven. "Repent", he preached, "for the kingdom of heaven is at hand". (2.) He tells them, that under the Gospel, carnal descent would profit them nothing. The subjects of the kingdom of heaven were, in this respect, not like branches in a tree, but like separate trees, each growing on its own root, to be preserved, or cut down, according to its fruits. (3.) He tells them, in particular, that their descent from Abraham would profit them nothing, ver. 9. (4.) He tells them that the axe was now laid to the root of the trees; that every tree which bringeth not forth good fruit is hewn down, and cast into the fire; that Christ's fan was in his hand; that the wheat must be gathered into the garner, but the chaff burned up with unquenchable fire. The language is figurative, but the meaning is plain,—Christ will judge men according to their personal character; this judgment is announced in his doctrine, and represented in his ordinances, and in the constitution and discipline of his churches.

From these observations, it appears that *the religion of the Gospel is personal, not hereditary.* If their descent from Abraham would not profit the Jews, much less can their descent from Noah, or their immediate parents, profit the Gentiles. Grace does not run in the blood; and a claim for baptism cannot be founded upon a qualification which does not exist.*

Carefully note Mark iii. 31—35; "There came then his brethren and his mother, and, standing

---

* Compare Luke iii. 8; John viii. 33—44.

without, sent unto him, calling him. And the multitude sat about him, and they said unto him, Behold, thy mother and thy brethren without seek for thee. And he answered them, saying, Who is my mother, or my brethren? And he looked round about on them which sat about him, and said, Behold my mother and my brethren! For whosoever shall do the will of God, the same is my brother, and my sister, and mother". Mary was a saint, and is now in heaven; but she is saved, not by her relation to our Lord as her son, but as her Saviour. The word "brethren" was used amongst the Jews in a sense more extended than amongst us; it was synonymous with the word "kindred." Some of our Lord's kindred were believers. "Have we not power to lead about a sister, a wife, as well as other apostles, and as the brethren of the Lord, and Cephas?": 1 Cor. ix. 5. Some of our Lord's kindred did not believe. "For neither did his brethren believe on him": John vii. 5. Such of our Lord's brethren as were saved, owed their salvation, not to their birth, but to their Saviour. The difference between those who believed and those who believed not, was not the effect of consanguinity. The importance of attending to this is indicated by the repetition of the narrative, which we find recorded by Matthew, Mark, and Luke. The truth which it inculcates is frequently stated. "For in Jesus Christ neither circumcision availeth anything, nor uncircumcision; but faith which worketh by love": Gal. v. 6. "Where there is neither Greek nor Jew, circumcision nor uncircumcision, Barbarian, Scythian, bond nor free: but Christ is all, and in all": Col. iii. 11. Again, in

Philip. iii. 3, 4: "We are the circumcision, which worship God in the spirit, and rejoice in Christ Jesus, and have no confidence in the flesh. Though I might also have confidence in the flesh. If any other man thinketh that he hath whereof he might trust in the flesh, I more."

It is not possible to state the doctrine in stronger or plainer language than that in which it is expressed by John (chap. i. 12, 13 :) "But as many as received him, to them gave he power to become the sons of God, even to them that believe on his name: which were born, not of blood, nor of the will of the flesh, nor of the will of man, but of God". "That is, children by a generation spiritual and divine, which has nothing in common with natural generation".—*Campbell*.

"They who thus believed on him were possessed of these privileges, not in consequence of their being born of blood, of their being descended from the loins of the holy patriarchs, or sharing in circumcision, and the blood of the sacrifices ; nor could they ascribe it merely to the will of the flesh, or to their own superior wisdom and goodness, as if by the power of corrupted nature alone they had made themselves to differ ; nor to the will of man, or to the wisest advice and most powerful exhortations which their fellow-creatures might address to them; but must humbly acknowledge that they were born of God, and indebted to the efficacious influences of his regenerating grace, for all their privileges, and for all their hopes."— *Doddridge*.

"We are born sons, not by virtue of the blood of circumcision, by which the Jews entered into covenant with God, and became his sons; not by reason of that carnal generation, which makes us sons by nature; not by the will of man, adopting another for his son for want of natural issue; but this sonship ariseth from the good pleasure of God, receiving us for his sons, through faith in Christ Jesus."—*Whitby*.

Other expositors agree with those quoted in explaining the words as referring our spiritual birth, not to our natural descent, but unto God.* To assert, in the face of this testimony, that infants derive spiritual benefit from natural descent, is rather to contradict than to explain the doctrines of revelation. Again, John iii. 5, 6: "Jesus answered, Verily, verily, I say unto thee, Except a man be born of water and of the Spirit, he cannot enter into the kingdom of God. That which is born of the flesh is flesh; and that which is born of the Spirit is spirit. Marvel not that I said unto thee, Ye must be born again". This testimony to the spiritual inutility of natural descent, though more full and more plain, exactly coincides with that of

---

* In this passage (John i. 12, 13,) the apostle contrasts the *one* way in which believers enjoy the privileges of the kingdom of heaven with the *three* ways in which men enjoyed the privileges of the Jewish dispensation: 1. By being born of blood, being descended from Abraham, Isaac, and Jacob. As it was not enough to be descended from Abraham, like Ishmael, or from Abraham and Isaac, like Esau, but from all the three patriarchs, the plural *bloods* is made use of. 2. By the will of the flesh, or submitting to the ordinance of circumcision: Ex. xii. 48, 49. 3. By the will of man: when the master by circumcision cast in his lot with Israel, all his males were circumcised, and then they might eat the passover, and although strangers, were under the same law as those who were born in the land.—J. H.

the Baptist. Nicodemus, no doubt, like the Pharisees and Sadducees, founded his hope on his Abrahamic blood: our Lord undeceives him. The expectant of the blessings of the kingdom of heaven (he tells him) must have another and better birth than that derived from the patriarchs. We must be born of the Spirit. Flesh, not spirit, is the product of natural birth: what is spiritual must be derived from the Spirit, not from carnal descent. "That which is born of the flesh is flesh; and that which is born of the Spirit is spirit. Marvel not that I said unto thee, Ye must be born again". "In plain terms, whosoever would become a subject of the kingdom of God, must not only be baptized, but must experience the renewing and sanctifying influences of the Holy Spirit on his soul. For were it possible for a man to be born again, by entering a second time into his mother's womb, such a second birth would do no more to qualify him for the kingdom of God than the first; for that which is born of the flesh is only flesh, and what proceeds and is produced from parents that are sinful and corrupt is sinful and corrupt as they are; but that which is born of the Spirit is formed to a resemblance of that blessed Spirit, whose office it is to infuse a Divine life into the soul".—*Doddridge.*

Other expositors give precisely the same explanation of the passage. Children, then, derive nothing spiritual from carnal descent. Again, Rom. ix. 7, 8: "Neither, because they are the seed of Abraham, are they all children; but in Isaac shall thy seed be called. That is, they which are the children of the flesh, these are not the children of

God: but the children of the promise are counted for the seed". Ver. 13: "As it is written, Jacob have I loved, but Esau have I hated". Esau and Jacob had the same blood, but a different spirit: both were the descendants of believing Isaac; and as descended from him, both were equally corrupt. The difference arose, not from descent, but from the promise. The apostle generalizes the doctrine: "They who are the children of the flesh, these are not the children of God." We have already seen, and shall soon see more fully, that the maxim is of universal application.

This passage, then, bears additional testimony to the truth that nothing spiritual is derived from carnal descent. Again, 2 Cor. v. 16, 17: "Wherefore, henceforth know we no man after the flesh; yea, though we have known Christ after the flesh, yet now henceforth know we him no more. Therefore if any man be in Christ, he is a new creature". "For this reason (that Christ died 'as the substitute of sinners of all nations,' ver. 15), therefore we, the ministers of the gospel of reconciliation, think ourselves bound to preach it to all nations, without regarding any man as better or worse on account of his pedigree and external privileges, or of his being circumcised in the flesh or not."—*Guise.*

"Wherefore, since Christ died for all, we, the apostles of Christ, from this time forth, in the exercise of our ministry, show respect to no man more than to another, on account of his being a Jew, according to the flesh, and even if we have formerly esteemed Christ on account of his being a

PRESUMPTIONS AGAINST INFANT BAPTISM. 103

Jew, yet now we esteem him no more on that account".—*Macknight.**

The sum of these comments is:—The apostles made no difference between the Jew and the Gentile, because the atonement was made for Gentiles as well as Jews. Judaism was founded in descent from the patriarchs. *Christianity is not founded in carnal relation of any kind.* It is not on carnal relation that its privileges depend; it is not on account of carnal relation that men are admitted to its ordinances; it is not in consequence of carnal relation that men are bound by its laws. There is no exception. No man is respected for his carnal descent. This passage does not indeed assert, in as many words, that children, infant or adult, are inadmissible to baptism from their relationship to their parents; it is, however, plainly implied. If we state the doctrine in an interrogatory form, this immediately appears. To whom should we have respect on account of carnal descent? Answer. To none; by consequence, not to children, whether infant or adult. In what concerns of Christianity are we to have respect to carnal descent? Answer. In none; by consequence, not in baptism.

I leave it to all to judge whether, in the passages now quoted, it be not plainly implied, that children, whether infant or adult, cannot be baptized in consequence of their relation to their parents. Again, Heb. viii. 8: "Behold, the days come, saith the

---

* Not knowing Christ after the flesh seems rather to mean, not knowing him as the Saviour of the Jews, in which character alone he was expected by the nation of Israel.—J. H.

Lord, when I will make a new covenant with the house of Israel and with the house of Judah: not according to the covenant that I made with their fathers in the day when I took them by the hand, to lead them out of the land of Egypt; because they continued not in my covenant, and I regarded them not, saith the Lord. For this is the covenant that I will make with the house of Israel after those days, saith the Lord; I will put my laws into their mind, and write them in their hearts; and I will be to them a God, and they shall be to me a people: and they shall not teach every man his neighbour, and every man his brother, saying, Know the Lord: for all shall know me, from the least to the greatest. For I will be merciful to their unrighteousness, and their sins and their iniquities will I remember no more". The doctrine of this passage is summary and conclusive. That this promise belongs not to all the infants of believers, the wicked lives of many of them in after years give decisive proof. The unavoidable consequence is,—they are not introduced into the new covenant by their carnal descent. All the children of believers are not taught of God; all the subjects of this covenant are taught of God. It is not, therefore, on their relation to believers, but on their spiritual relation to Christ, that they are entitled to the benefits or ordinances of the Gospel.

Again, 1 Pet. i. 23, 24: "Being born again, not of corruptible seed, but of incorruptible, by the word of God, which liveth and abideth for ever. For all flesh is as grass, and all the glory of man as the flower of grass. The grass withereth, and the flower thereof falleth away: but the word of the

Lord endureth for ever. And this is the word which by the gospel is preached unto you". These verses, almost in as many words, teach the doctrine for which we contend. Peter is treating of the cause of regeneration. He denies that it is by corruptible seed; he asserts that it is by the incorruptible seed of the word. The corruptible seed is carnal descent; it is corruptible because all flesh is grass. The incorruptible is the word of God, or the Gospel; it is incorruptible because it liveth and endureth for ever. Repeat these words I may, but I cannot make them plainer. Two or three quotations from friends of infant baptism may satisfy the inquirer that there is nothing peculiar in this explanation.

"The temper and conduct which I recommend may justly be expected from you, considering your relation to God and to each other: as having been regenerated, not by corruptible seed, not by virtue of any descent from human parents, but by incorruptible; not laying the stress of your confidence on your pedigree from Abraham, if ye had the honour to descend from that illustrious patriarch, for that descent could not entitle you to the important blessings of the Gospel. It is by means of the efficacy of the word of God upon your hearts, even that powerful word, which lives and endures for ever, that you are become entitled to these glorious evangelical privileges".—*Doddridge.*

"In this expression, the apostle insinuated to the Jews, that they were not the children of God and heirs of immortality, by their being begotten of Abraham, nor by their obeying the law of Moses, but by their being begotten of the incorruptible seed of the preached word of the living God."—*Macknight*.

This testimony, then, almost in so many words, proves that infants cannot be baptized on account of their descent. Again, under the Old Dispensation, the temporal interests of the child were judicially affected by the conduct of the parent. Of this we have an example in Exod. xx. 5: "For I the Lord thy God am a jealous God, visiting the iniquity of the fathers upon the children unto the third and fourth generation of them that hate me; and showing mercy unto thousands of them that love me, and keep my commandments".

It is not perhaps implied in the words quoted, but certainly often and plainly predicted by the prophets, that under the Gospel this constitution of things should be altered. Under that dispensation, the temporal interests, and much less the spiritual interests of the child, are in no judicial way affected by the conduct of the parent. Both directly and indirectly, the prophecies confirm the truth, that the child derives no spiritual privilege from his lineage. "In those days they shall say no more, The fathers have eaten a sour grape, and the children's teeth are set on edge. But every one shall die for his own iniquity: every man that eateth the sour grape, his teeth shall be set on edge. Behold, the days come, saith the Lord, that I will make a new covenant with the house of Israel, and with the house of Judah": Jer. xxxi. 29—31. "What mean ye, that ye use this proverb concerning the land of Israel, saying, The fathers have eaten sour grapes, and the children's teeth are set on edge? As I live, saith the Lord God, ye shall not have occasion any more to use this proverb in Israel". * Ezek. xviii. 2, 3.

Thus it appears that the right to baptism does not run in blood, and we ought also to be satisfied that infants cannot be baptized in consequence of their descent from their parents, whether more immediate or more remote.

---

* The difference between the Old and New Covenants is exhibited by a passage which refers to the restoration of Israel: Is. xxvii. 12. "And it shall come to pass in that day, that the Lord shall beat off from the channel of the river unto the stream of Egypt, and ye shall be gathered *one by one*, O ye children of Israel." The *nation* of Israel had been cast off for the breach of the Sinai covenant, as the Lord says by Jeremiah, "which my covenant they brake, and I regarded them not", but they are to be "gathered one by one", by a new and better covenant, which cannot be national, but individual, because by it the law of God is written upon the heart of every child of the covenant. The nation may be born in a day, but it must be by an individual process. The same thing is taught by Ezek. xvi. 61—63. Sodom and Samaria (representing the Gentiles), the sisters of Jerusalem in wickedness, are to be given unto her for daughters, "but not by thy covenant."—J. H.

LECTURE X.

FURTHER PRESUMPTIONS AGAINST INFANT BAPTISM.

VII. A seventh presumption against infant baptism arises from ITS INCONGRUITY WITH THE ANALOGY OF FAITH.

Christianity is a system: its parts, adapted to one another, form a consistent whole. To prove that any doctrine or practice agrees not with other doctrines and duties of Christianity, is to prove that it is not a Christian doctrine or practice at all. If I prove that Pædo-baptism accords not with the analogy of the truth as it is in Jesus, I prove, or at least I bring a strong presumption, that it is not a Christian institute.

1. *Infant baptism does not accord with the scripture doctrine of election.* The Scriptures teach us that election is the divine choice of persons to eternal life, and not the choice of tribes or of families. "For whom he did foreknow, he also did predestinate to be conformed to the image of his Son, that he might be the firstborn among many brethren. Moreover whom he did predestinate, them he also called; and whom he called, them he also justified; and whom he justified, them he also glorified": Rom. viii. 29, 30. This is a description, not of families and tribes, but of persons called and

saved. "All that the Father giveth me shall come to me; and him that cometh to me, I will in no wise cast out. And this is the Father's will which hath sent me, that of all which he hath given me I should lose nothing, but should raise it up again at the last day": John vi. 37, 39. This election is personal and saving. "As thou hast given him power over all flesh, that he should give eternal life to as many as thou hast given him": John xvii. 2. "I pray for them; I pray not for the world, but for them which thou hast given me, for they are thine": Ver. 9. "Father, I will that they also, whom thou hast given me, be with me where I am, that they may behold my glory": Ver. 24. "Notwithstanding, in this rejoice not, that the spirits are subject unto you; but rather rejoice because your names are written in heaven": Luke x. 20. "And all that dwell upon the earth shall worship him, whose names are not written in the book of life of the Lamb slain from the foundation of the world": Rev. xiii. 8. "And I entreat thee also, true yokefellow, help those women which laboured with me in the gospel, with Clement also, and with other my fellow-labourers, whose names are in the book of life": Phil. iv. 3. "For the children being not yet born, neither having done any good or evil, that the purpose of God according to election might stand, not of works, but of him that calleth; it was said unto her, The elder shall serve the younger. As it is written, Jacob have I loved, but Esau have I hated": Rom. ix. 11—13.

On the supposition that infants derive some spiritual and saving benefit from their birth or baptism, they would be saved by families, by tribes, by nations; whereas the election of the Bible is neither an election of nations, nor tribes, nor families, but of persons only, to salvation. But the fact renders this incongruity still more glaring. Every one of the scriptures just quoted connects election with salvation. But who, that looks at their wicked lives and impenitent deaths, is not painfully convinced that many of those baptized in infancy are not finally saved? In the first passage quoted on this particular, it is asserted, and in all the rest it is supposed, that saving grace is inseparably connected with glory. If the infants of believers derive grace from their birth or baptism, and lose it before they die, he must be very inattentive, indeed, who observes not the incongruity referred to. Throughout the world called Christian the great body of the people are baptized, or sprinkled in infancy. On the supposition that birth and baptism convey saving grace, the number of the elect greatly exceeds the number of the called. The doctrine of the Scriptures is just the reverse. In Matt. xx. 16, and frequently elsewhere, we are told that "many are called, but few chosen". These remarks more immediately interest that numerous class of Pædo-baptists who suppose that grace is conferred by blood, or by baptism; but they are uninteresting to none. They must prove fatal, like those which follow, to pædo-baptism, until it be proved, as it never will, that, like circumcision, it stands on scripture precept or example, and, like it, has no personal respect to the subject. The inquirer may examine for himself. Is it supposed that baptism imparts any temporal good? The supposition is contradicted by fact:

the baptized are neither more healthy, more wealthy, nor longer lived than others; nay, many of them die in infancy. Is it supposed that infants derive spiritual good from their birth or baptism? The supposition contradicts all the Scriptures quoted, and many more which might have been quoted to the same purpose.

2. *Infant baptism is inconsistent with the doctrine of representation.* In the popular worship, every parent is the representative of his children, immediate, remote, or both; hence there are as many representatives as there are parents. But is this the Scripture doctrine of representation? It is very different. Adam, the first man, represented all his posterity, descending from him by ordinary generation. Christ, the second man, represents the election. Of these two representatives we read in Scripture. It is as representatives that Adam is called the first, and Christ the second man: Rom. v. 19. "For as by one man's disobedience many were made sinners, so by the obedience of one shall many be made righteous." Adam and Christ are meant. Of other representatives the Scripture makes no mention, and by its silence excludes them. The exclusion of all moral representatives, (Christ and Adam excepted,) is most explicitly taught in the passage just quoted. Many men intervened between Adam and Christ; but from Adam to Christ there was no moral representative. All parents, Abraham not excepted, are excluded from this honour. "By the obedience of *one* shall many be made righteous": it is by the obedience of Christ, exclusive of the obedience of others. If the child be justified at all, he is

justified by the righteousness of Christ exclusively; the righteousness of the parent is excluded.

The recollection of these things will dissipate the clouds which ignorance and design have gathered around this subject, from the covenants with Abraham, David, and others. They are expressly excluded from moral representation; they were merely typical representatives. To assert that the moral condition of infants depends on their blood or their baptism is to oppose the Scriptures, as in many other respects, so particularly in respect of representation. This incongruity attaches to all Pædo-baptists who found baptism in parentage.

3. *Infant baptism is inconsistent with the covenant of grace, or covenant of God.* The Scripture doctrine on this topic is as follows:—All mankind, descending from Adam by ordinary generation, have fallen by the apostasy of their representative into an estate of sin and misery. "By the offence of one, judgment came upon all men to condemnation": Rom. v. 18. God from eternity selected a number of our fallen race, and gave them to his Son, the Lord Jesus Christ, to be redeemed by him. "According as he hath chosen us in him before the foundation of the world": Eph. i. 4. In the time and manner appointed by God, the redeemed become acquainted with the gospel, and are made to believe it. This blessing flows from the grace of God, and is communicated by the regenerating work of the Holy Ghost. "Not by works of righteousness which we have done, but according to his mercy he saved us, by the washing of regeneration, and renewing of the Holy Ghost": Titus iii. 5. "For by grace are ye saved through

faith, and that not of yourselves; it is the gift of God": Eph. ii. 8. By this faith they are united to Christ, brought personally into covenant with God, and interested in all our Lord's merits and benefits. " But of him are ye in Christ Jesus, who of God is made unto us wisdom, and righteousness, and sanctification, and redemption": 1 Cor. i. 30.

Such is the account we receive from the Scriptures of the covenant of grace. The process by which infants are supposed to be brought into the covenant of baptism or sprinkling is generally known, and need not be recapitulated. Let it only be recollected that many or most of the sprinkled come short of holiness and happiness, and the incongruity will immediately appear. In the covenant of grace all is ordered and sure, as the purpose of God on which it rests. In the covenant of infant baptism or of sprinkling all is precarious. In the covenant of grace there is one, and but one, representative. In the covenant of baptism or sprinkling there are others—parents or sponsors, or both. Into the covenant of grace men are brought by the Spirit: parents or sponsors bring infants into the covenant of baptism or sprinkling. Faith alone is the medium of interest in the covenant of grace: infants are brought into the covenant of sprinkling by birth, baptism, or by what is termed common grace. Men in covenant with God have all the benefits of the covenant of grace—justification, adoption, sanctification, with all their consequences, here and hereafter: many or most baptized or sprinkled infants enjoy none of these benefits. Everything is personal in the covenant of grace: in the covenant of sprinkling there is nothing personal whatever.

Before concluding this particular, permit me to press these remarks on the attention of such as speak of bringing infants, by baptism or sprinkling, into covenant with God. Such would do well to consider what covenant they mean. If the covenant of grace be intended, the incongruities referred to demonstrate that they are mistaken. Men are neither given to nor interested in Christ by baptism. The elect were given to Christ before the foundation of the world; and the mystical union in time is formed, not by baptism, but by faith. If some other covenant be intended, it ought to be recollected that, under the gospel, no covenant exists but the covenant of grace. The typical covenants, with all that concerns them, have answered their purposes, and ceased. Infants, therefore, can be brought into no covenant by baptism. Should the inquirer ask how elect infants are saved? he must be reminded, that the Scriptures do not furnish us with a positive answer; they do teach us, however, that they are not saved by baptism or by immediate descent. The great proportion of those who die in infancy are descended from Heathens or Mahommedans, and have no baptism. This fact is not a little instructive in practice. The best interests of infants sustain no loss, either by their descent from unbelieving parents, or by their want of baptism.

4. *Infant baptism is inconsistent with the perpetuity of saving grace.* Some found infant baptism on common grace, that is, communications supposed to be made to all men, which save whilst retained, but which may be forfeited and lost. Though this fiction be avowed by Arminians only, it seems in

PRESUMPTIONS AGAINST INFANT BAPTISM.

some degree to be adopted by many, if not all, who adhere to the popular practice. Baptism is considered a privilege, and the want of it a prejudice to the souls of infants. Hence, those who practise infant baptism are supposed to deal more kindly with their children than those who maintain that it is a piece of unauthorised will-worship. The mortifying fact must, however, be recollected, that many persons baptized in infancy never attain to holiness or heaven. If they be justified in baptism, the sentence is afterwards reversed, for eventually they are condemned. If they were sanctified, their sanctifying grace has perished; they live and die impenitent. But is this the doctrine of the Bible? The apostle, in Rom. viii. 38, 39, teaches us that the sentence of justification is irrevocable. "For I am persuaded that neither death, nor life, nor angels, nor principalities, nor powers, nor things present, nor things to come, nor height, nor depth, nor any other creature, shall be able to separate us from the love of God, which is in Christ Jesus our Lord." The perseverance of the sanctified is no less plainly asserted. "I will make an everlasting covenant with them, that I will not turn away from them, to do them good; but I will put my fear in their hearts, that they shall not depart from me": Jer. xxxii. 40. "Whosoever drinketh of the water that I shall give him shall never thirst; but the water that I shall give him shall be in him a well of water, springing up into everlasting life": John iv. 14. "My sheep hear my voice, and I know them, and they follow me: and I give unto them eternal life; and they shall never perish, neither shall any pluck them out of my hand" John x. 27. Believers are "kept by the power of God, through faith, unto salvation, ready to be revealed in the last time": 1 Pet. i. 5. "Whosoever is born of God doth not commit sin; for his seed remaineth in him: and he cannot sin, because he is born of God": 1 John iii. 9. "These things have I written unto you that believe on the name of the Son of God; that ye may know that ye have eternal life, and that ye may believe on the name of the Son of God": 1 John v. 13. So plain is the doctrine of the Scriptures, that, as Paul tells us, "The gifts and calling of God are without repentance": Rom xi. 29, and proportionately plain is the incongruity of infant baptism with this doctrine.

It might be of much use to such as practise the ceremony to determine the exact nature of the benefit received in it. If grace be received, facts appear to show that in most cases it is afterwards lost. But this, we have seen, is contrary to the analogy of Scripture. The Scriptures everywhere teach the perpetuity of grace. If nothing be received, it cannot be an institution of God. The service is illusory and vain; and it will not be easy to vindicate it from the charge of profanity. The name of Jehovah is solemnly pronounced about nothing. "The Lord will not hold him guiltless that taketh his name in vain."

5. *Infant baptism tends, in direct opposition to the Scriptures, to confound the Church with the world.* In national churches, the fact is notorious, acknowledged, and unavoidable. In them the Church is a geographical idea; all within certain

bounds are born, sprinkled, and reared within her pale. Individuals in Established Churches, not aware of the restraints under which they are placed, have often attempted to remedy the evil; their attempts, however, have uniformly failed, and by their failure have given experimental evidence of the invincible repugnance of these institutions to the laws of Christ. The case is similar in all societies of consistent Pædobaptists; for example, the Greek and Eastern Churches admit infants to the Lord's supper. The generality of infants, as appears from their after lives, belong to the world. In these communions, therefore, the Church and the world are systematically confounded by means of baptizing infants. Some communions admit infants to sprinkling, whilst they reject them from the Supper. This conduct is inconsistent; for if the faith of the parent give his child a right to the one ordinance, it cannot fail to give him a right to the other. In neither case does the right depend on personal, but on relative qualifications. Personally, the infant is qualified for neither ordinance; relatively, he is qualified for both, if qualified for either.

I said that those who make a distinction between infant baptism and infant communion are inconsistent; but the evil of confounding the Church with the world is not remedied by the inconsistency. Have we not good grounds to conclude, both from reason and observation, that in societies which follow this practice, applications for communion will be made and admitted more readily, than in those churches in which each member is received, after being baptized on a credible profession of repentance towards God, and of faith towards the Lord Jesus Christ. Thus the first part of our assertion is proved, that infant baptism tends to confound the church with the world.

I now observe that *this confusion is condemned by the Scriptures.* The evidence here is multiplied and strong. I shall quote but a few texts. All the members of the primitive churches are described as called, elected, sanctified, adopted, heirs of God and of glory. Men of a different character, if we are guided by primitive example, are neither to be admitted into church communion, nor retained in it, if admitted. "Moreover, if thy brother shall trespass against thee, go and tell him his fault between thee and him alone: if he shall hear thee, thou hast gained thy brother. But if he will not hear thee, then take with thee one or two more, that in the mouth of two or three witnesses every word may be established. And if he shall neglect to hear them, tell it unto the church; but if he neglect to hear the church, let him be unto thee as an heathen man and a publican": Matt. xviii. 15—17. "Now we command you, brethren, in the name of our Lord Jesus Christ, that ye withdraw yourselves from every brother that walketh disorderly, and not after the tradition which he received of us": 2 Thess. iii. 6. Compare these and many like Scriptures, with the descriptions of positive goodness required in the members of churches, and the care of Christ to keep and preserve the Church in separation from the world will appear. No one who is not born of water and of the Spirit can lawfully enter these holy societies, or continue in them.

The repugnance of infant baptism, both in spirit and effect, to the purity of church communion, furnishes another incongruity with the analogy of the faith so strong, that if a positive appointment of the practice cannot be produced, we must conclude that the popular system forms no part of the revelation of God. In many particulars, infant baptism transgresses the analogy of Scripture. I can name but a few of them. Infant baptism accords not with the grand design of the plan of redemption, to show the exceeding riches of his grace, in his kindness towards his people, through Christ Jesus. Eph. ii. 7. In this ceremony, descent, common grace, or the operation itself, either supplants or determines grace. The religion of the New Testament is a personal thing. The believer owes his privileges to no relative but Christ. Infant baptism, on the contrary, is altogether relative; everything personal is, from the nature of the case, excluded.

Infant baptism accords not with faith as the medium of receiving the benefits of redemption. In the Scriptures faith is everything; in infant baptism it is nothing; descent, common grace, or the mere act of sprinkling is substituted for faith. "But we speak of infants," say some. Be it so. Infant sprinkling accords as little with the manner in which Heathen and Mahommedan infants are saved as with that by which believers are saved. In what manner the merits of Christ are applied in cases like these the Scriptures do not inform us; but be it what it may, it is neither by descent from godly parents nor baptism; so that here, again, infant sprinkling does not accord with God's ordinary way of saving infants. Few, I apprehend, will be disposed to believe that all Heathen, Mahommedan, and other unbaptized infants, are damned because they have not been sprinkled or baptized, and yet we might well tremble for them if salvation could only come to them by infant baptism.

Again, *the common ceremony accords not with the doctrine of original sin.* At what age our race passes out of a state of infancy into a state of personal responsibility, I cannot tell; but at what time soever the transition be made, it is made, on the principles of Pædo-baptists, with special advantages on the part of the sprinkled. They are supposed to derive these advantages from godly descent or sprinkling. Heathen and Mahommedan infants can derive nothing from these sources. Compare, on the principles of Pædo-baptists, these two classes of infants; and observe that the sprinkled, and the descendants of professors, become a privileged order. But what is the doctrine of the Scriptures? Everyone who has read them can judge for himself. Is original sin, with its consequences, restricted to one class more than to another? Did it ever occur to us that some infants passed into a state of personal responsibility with greater inherent advantages than others? Yet it must be the case if baptism is to be understood upon the Pædo-baptist theory.

To conclude: the more closely we examine the subject, the more evident does it appear that infant baptism is inconsistent with Christianity. Had we proof, by precept, by example, or in any other way, that infant baptism is the will of God, we would submit our reasonings to revelation and sprinkle our infants. But if no proof to this effect can be produced, and if infant baptism clashes (as we have seen that it does), with most of the fundamental doctrines of our holy religion, what should a candid and conscientious man do, when the presumption appears so strong, that infant baptism belongs not to that system, with which it is so palpably incongruous?

VIII. An eighth presumption against infant sprinkling arises from THE PERSONAL INTEREST OF THE BAPTIZED IN THE THINGS REPRESENTED IN BAPTISM.

1. The objects represented in baptism are facts, doctrines, duties, privileges. For the present I speak of *privileges*, and shall attempt to prove that the privileges represented are *saving*. "He that believeth and is baptized shall be saved; but he that believeth not shall be damned": Mark xvi. 16. The privilege here is salvation. This privilege is received by faith, and the reception is represented by baptism. "Now when they heard this, they were pricked in their heart, and said unto Peter and to the rest of the apostles, Men and brethren, what shall we do? Then Peter said unto them, Repent, and be baptized every one of you in the name of Jesus Christ for the remission of sins, and ye shall receive the gift of the Holy Ghost. Then they that gladly received his word were baptized": Acts. ii. 37, 38, 41. "And now why tarriest thou? arise, and be baptized, and wash away thy sins, calling on the name of the Lord": Acts xxii. 16. Peter tells his hearers, and Ananias tells Paul, that

remission of sins is exhibited in baptism. But remission of sins is a saving benefit. "Whom he justified, them he also glorified": Rom. viii. 30. Adoption is received by faith, and represented in baptism. "For ye are all the children of God by faith in Christ Jesus. For as many of you as have been baptized into Christ, have put on Christ": Gal. iii. 26, 27. Sanctification is exhibited in baptism. "According to his mercy he saved us, by the washing of regeneration, and renewing of the Holy Ghost": Titus iii. 5. Regeneration is saving, and is represented in baptism. "The like figure whereunto even baptism doth also now save us (not the putting away the filth of the flesh, but the answer of a good conscience toward God,) by the resurrection of Christ": 1 Pet. iii. 21.

These, and many other Scriptures, prove the truth of our first assertion, that baptism exhibits saving benefits, and represents the believer's participation in these benefits. It, therefore, differs from circumcision, to which multitudes were entitled without partaking of any spiritual blessing. Salvation, on the contrary, is the infallible portion of every individual who has obtained precious faith in the righteousness of Christ; in other words, in the doctrine into which he is baptized. A hypocrite may be baptized and perish; but this does not affect the truth, that where the profession made in baptism is sincere it is inseparably connected with the salvation which it represents. It is the profession of the believer's faith in the death, burial, and resurrection of Christ, and of his being by his resurrection begotten to a lively hope of an inheritance incorruptible, undefiled, and which fadeth not away. Nothing external can secure salvation. The kingdom of God is "righteousness, and peace, and joy in the Holy Ghost": it is within us: Rom xiv. 17; Luke xvii. 21. But baptism is the appointed means of putting on Christ; of assuming his livery; of going forth to him without the gate; the sign of our having begun to look for a better country beyond the grave, even an heavenly.

The design of the ordinance, therefore, namely, to represent the personal interest of the baptized in the salvation of Christ, must prevent its being administered to infants. " But ought not infants, for the same reason, to have been kept from circumcision ?" I answer, no. The design of circumcision was totally different from the design of baptism. Circumcision, except in the case of Abraham, was never designed to represent saving benefits as the privilege of the circumcised. It was the token of the covenant with Abraham that Christ should spring from his loins, and that the promise in all its parts should be fulfilled in the salvation of those who possessed the faith of Abraham. "And he received the sign of circumcision, a seal of the righteousness of the faith which he had yet being uncircumcised, that he might be the father of all them that believe, though they be not circumcised; that righteousness might be imputed unto them also: and the father of circumcision to them who are not of the circumcision only, but who also walk in the steps of that faith of our father Abraham, which he had yet being uncircumcised. For the promise, that he should be the heir of the world, was not to Abraham or to his seed, through the law, but through the righteousness of faith": Rom. iv. 11—13.

The rite represented no saving benefit to the infant. The infant's body was like the canvas on which the truths were painted. The sign was calculated to remind the spectator, and the circumcised himself, when capable of observing it, of all the precious promises of the covenant, and particularly of the history of the patriarch as the pattern of faith and hope. As soon as the circumcised believed, he might, by the sign, be confirmed in his hope of salvation. Till then he could have no such assurance. Circumcision was not a sign of righteousness by descent; it was a sign of righteousness by faith. As to what chiefly concerns us, I said that the infant's body was merely the canvas, on which the truths of the Gospel were drawn. Circumcision answered this purpose on whomsoever the operation was performed. The correctness of these statements appears from the facts. By the commandment of God, circumcision was administered to Ishmael as well as to Isaac; to the sons of Keturah, whatever was their moral character; to male Israelites and proselytes, believing and unbelieving, without distinction.*

---

* God promised to Abraham to be a God to him and to his seed; the apostle tells us, "he saith not to seeds as of many, but as of one; and to thy seed, which is Christ," (Gal. iii. 16); consequently Isaac alone, the child of promise, the progenitor and type of Christ, was interested in the Abrahamic covenant, and this was intimated by Ishmael and the six sons of Keturah being sent out of the family. The Lord refers to this, when he says, (John viii. 35,) "And the servant abideth not in the house for ever: but the Son abideth ever." Ishmael, the son of the bond-woman, was the type of Israel after the flesh, (Gal. iv. 25,) who, like him, were cast out of Abraham's house; he does not acknowledge the unbelieving Jews, Is. lxiii. 16.—J. H.

In every instance, circumcision was a seal of the righteousness of faith, by which Abraham was justified in uncircumcision. Hence we may see that in no instance, with the exception of Abraham, did it represent saving benefits as the privilege of the circumcised, as baptism does to every baptized believer. If I have made myself understood; the reason is plain why infants might be circumcised under the law, whilst they may not be baptized under the Gospel Dispensation.

LECTURE XI.

CONCLUDING PRESUMPTIONS AGAINST INFANT BAPTISM.

IX. A ninth presumption against infant-baptism arises from THE GREATER CERTAINTY OF BELIEVER-BAPTISM.

Supposing, for a moment, that it were doubtful whether infants ought or ought not to be baptized, yet, even on this supposition, believer-baptism would be our duty. It is an established rule, in all doubtful cases to take the safer side. Let the following things be considered, and it will appear that it is more safe to practise believer-baptism than infant-sprinkling.

1. *We must be baptized.* This position needs no proof; it is confirmed by doctrines, examples, and precepts. "If thou shalt confess with thy mouth the Lord Jesus, and shalt believe in thine heart that God hath raised him from the dead, thou shalt be saved. For with the heart man believeth unto righteousness; and with the mouth confession is made unto salvation": Rom. x. 9, 10. Of this profession, baptism is the symbol. "Jesus answered, Verily, verily, I say unto thee, Except a man be born of water and of the Spirit, he cannot enter into the kingdom of God": John iii. 5.

2. *The same subject cannot be baptized in more ways than one.* Suppose a parent in deliberation

whether a child is to be baptized on his descent or on his faith, it would immediately occur to him that the one of these practices excludes the other; whichever he prefers, the other is rejected. The doctrine of the Scriptures on this head seems to be admitted by all. Baptism is not to be repeated. It is because infant baptism is a nullity, that believers are immersed on their faith.

3. *The evidence for infant sprinkling is confessedly doubtful;* there is neither precept nor example in support of the practice. It must be allowed that the inferences adduced in its support are all questionable. There is not one of these inferences which has not, by one or other of its ablest abettors, been rejected as inconclusive. Many observe the ceremony without scruple and possibly with great confidence; but in these cases it is generally known that the subject has not been examined. Whoever pleases may make the experiment. Let him name his reason for adopting the practice, he will find that his plea has been rejected by some of the friends of sprinkling. Ingenuity has been questioned on the rack; her answers are exhausted.

4. *The evidence for believer-baptism is unexceptionable:* it has never been rejected by any who did not reject the ordinance itself. The baptized assert, and the abettors of sprinkling deny, that whether sprinkled in infancy or not, every one, after believing, ought to be baptized: but neither deny that adults not sprinkled in infancy ought to be sprinkled or baptized. All missionaries baptize or sprinkle their adult converts, so satisfactory is the evidence for believer-baptism.

The deliberation is now brought to an issue. If my child shall be baptized on his faith, his baptism is scriptural and valid: if I shall sprinkle him on account of his descent, the case is very different. The reality of his baptism, as well as the morality of my own deed, must at best remain doubtful. The safer side is to postpone this questionable ceremony. It need hardly be mentioned, that these conclusions affect the man baptized in infancy as much as the parent. If infant baptism be questionable (may he say), my own baptism is questionable: respecting the validity of believer-baptism there can be no doubt; and there can be as little that I must make sure of being baptized. I must choose the safer side; and if I am a believer, it is my duty to be baptized.

X. Another presumption against infant sprinkling arises from THE INSPIRED DESCRIPTION OF THE MEMBERS OF THE NEW DISPENSATION.

The members of the New Dispensation are particularly described, both in the Old Testament and in the New. I shall give two or three of these descriptions from the New Testament. "Jesus answered and said unto Nicodemus, Verily, verily, I say unto thee, Except a man be born again, he cannot see the kingdom of God. Nicodemus saith unto him, How can a man be born when he is old? can he enter the second time into his mother's womb, and be born? Jesus answered, Verily, verily, I say unto thee, except a man be born of water and of the Spirit, he cannot enter into the kingdom of God": John iii. 3—5. It is generally allowed, that by the new birth regeneration is understood. In the context our Lord describes this change by the first actings of the new nature, namely, believing the record of God respecting his Son,—" For God so loved the world, that he gave his only-begotten Son, that whosoever believeth in him should not perish, but have everlasting life ": verse 16. The words are parallel to Mark xvi. 15, 16: " Go ye into all the world, and preach the Gospel to every creature. He that believeth and is baptized shall be saved, but he that believeth not shall be damned". It deserves particular notice, that regeneration evidencing itself in faith, stands opposed to natural descent. " That which is born of the flesh is flesh ; and that which is born of the Spirit is spirit. Marvel not that I said unto thee, Ye must be born again ": John iii. 6, 7. Our Lord is evidently speaking of the subjects of the Gospel Dispensation. He describes them positively. They are born of the Spirit: they give evidence of the change by believing and professing the faith. He describes them negatively: " That which is born of the flesh is flesh ". Both directly and indirectly, infants are excluded. In this respect the kingdom of heaven differs from the Old Dispensation. In the latter, men enjoyed all the privileges of the national covenant by birth; in the former, those privileges are limited to those who are born again.

The subjects of the New Dispensation are described in terms both negative and positive. They are all taught of God, from the least to the greatest. Hebrews viii. 11.

We have a third description of the subjects of the Gospel Dispensation in the preaching of John the Baptist, as recorded in Matt. iii. 8, 9. He is evidently referring to the last chapter of Malachi; and comparing the words of the Prophet with the words of the Baptist, we have another description of the visible subjects of the Gospel Dispensation. They must " bring forth fruits meet for repentance ". These descriptions necessarily exclude infants. "Think not to say within yourselves, We have Abraham to our father ".

The transaction recorded in Matt. xix. 13—15, Mark x. 13—16, and Luke xviii. 15—17, in no way opposes this doctrine. The words are these:— " And they brought unto him also infants, that he would touch them: but when his disciples saw it, they rebuked them. But Jesus called them unto him, and said, Suffer the little children to come unto me, and forbid them not: for of such is the kingdom of God. Verily, I say unto you, Whosoever shall not receive the kingdom of God as a little child, shall in no wise enter therein ". The words, " of *such* is the kingdom of God," may be referred either to the persons, or to the character of these infants. If we refer the words to the *character* of the children, the meaning will be this:—The subjects of the kingdom of heaven are, like these little children, humble and teachable. It was the manner of our Lord to seize such opportunities of conveying instruction: and the context favours this exposition. "Verily I say unto you, Whosoever shall not receive the kingdom of God as a little child, shall in no wise enter therein": Luke xviii. 17. If we refer the words, " of *such* is the kingdom of God," to the *persons* of these infants, the meaning will be this:—

Infants, like these, shall go to heaven. Taken in this sense, they do not warrant the admission of infants to baptism or to the Supper. They intimate no more than the fact that infants are saved. Infants may belong to the kingdom of God though they are neither admitted to baptism nor to the Supper. These infants were not brought to be baptized :—" And they brought young children to him that he should *touch* them ". They were not baptized :—" And he laid his hands on them, and departed thence": Mark x. 16. Whether they were, or were not, the children of believers we are not told ; nor are we told by whom they were brought. Not a word is spoken of infant baptism or sprinkling, though the opportunity was most favourable. We conclude, therefore, that this transaction furnishes no exception to the general rule ; and as the inspired descriptions of the members of the New Dispensation are inapplicable to infants, the presumption is that infants cannot be admitted to baptism or to the Supper.

XI. THE INUTILITY OF INFANT BAPTISM furnishes another presumption against it.

Infant sprinkling is useless: it is useless to infants, and to all others. Though we could discover no advantage attending it, either to infants, parents, or others, yet would it be our duty to practise it if thereby God were glorified. Obedience is honourable to God, but will-worship is not so. " Why are ye subject to ordinances . . after the commandments and doctrines of men ? " Col. ii. 20. Infant baptism is useless to infants ; they cannot enjoy any advantage communicated through the exercise of the mind, being incapable of mental operation. The only good which they can be supposed to derive from sprinkling, is that ascribed to baptism by Papists and others, namely, regenerating grace. Their natures might, no doubt, be sanctified as well at baptism as at death. But if two things be considered, all must be satisfied that baptismal regeneration is a fiction. Consider, first, the perpetuity of grace; and, secondly, the hopeless deaths of many or most of those sprinkled in infancy who live to riper years. They die without grace. Grace, therefore, they never had; that is, they were not regenerated in baptism. Now, there is no other conceivable good which infants are capable of deriving from baptism or sprinkling.

I said that it is also useless to parents, and to all others. But this must be proved; for it has been asserted that the utility of infant sprinkling is obvious; that it illustrates certain doctrines; and that to parents in particular it confirms the promises made in the Scriptures to themselves and to their children. This assertion is plausible, but fallacious. To detect the fallacy, it must be observed that the design, as well as the institution of ordinances, must be learned from revelation. I am no more at liberty to assign to an ordinance an unscriptural use, than I am to use a ceremony which God has not instituted. By misapplication to unwarranted ends an ordinance of God is profaned. The Bible itself is profaned when applied to superstitious purposes. Let it be observed, that nowhere in the Scripture is baptism represented as the symbol of the doctrines specified, nor once used to confirm promises either to parents or children. All the uses assigned to infant baptism are the creatures of imagination. Not a single text has been, or can be, produced in support of them. All sober Christians justly reprobate the practice of directing procedure by texts of Scripture at which we happen to open the Bible: for the same reason must the judicious inquirer reprobate as superstitions the idea of deriving instruction or comfort from the unsanctioned practice of infant baptism. Thus, in every view of the subject, infant baptism is useless. Now, it will require but little attention to be convinced that the ordinances of God are of a very different character. Every doctrine, every precept, every ordinance of God, is useful. The doctrines of Scripture are doctrines according to godliness. "More to be desired are the statutes of the Lord than gold, yea, than much fine gold." The ordinances are means of grace. Few need to be told the scriptural use of preaching or reading, of praying or communicating. In a word, what is said of the Scriptures collectively, is in its measure true of every part of their contents: "All Scripture is given by inspiration of God, and is profitable for doctrine, for reproof, for correction, for instruction in righteousness, that the man of God may be perfect, throughly furnished unto all good works": 2 Tim. iii. 16, 17. This is obviously true of believer-baptism; its uses are revealed, and often enforced.

Compare, now, what we have heard of divine ordinances with what has been proved of infant baptism, and the presumption against its divine origin strikingly appears. Of every one of the ordinances of God, the scriptural use can be stated:

but as to the use of infant baptism the Scriptures are totally silent. In observing the former, God is honoured and obeyed; the latter is will-worship. The appointments of the one are suited to the faculties of the worshippers; the mental faculties of unconscious infants are incapable of exercise. All the ordinances of God are calculated for edification: infant baptism is equally useless to infants, to parents, to him who administers, and to those who witness the ceremony. The presumption is confirmed; infant baptism is useless, and consequently not an ordinance of God.

XII. Another presumption against infant baptism is suggested by THE DESIGN OF BAPTISM.

The design of baptism, though deeply interesting, has seldom been exhibited according to its importance. My present object does not require a full statement of that design: some of its parts come afterwards to be noticed, but its general design must at present be opened, because, taking the revelation of its history as we have it, that general design affords a presumption against infant baptism. What, then, is the general design of baptism? *Answer*. Baptism is designed to represent the truth as applied to, and as received by, the baptized. It is designed to distinguish the recipient of the truth from such as never heard it, or who heard it without receiving it. Christ's commission to his apostles, (Matt. xxviii.) gives a statement of the general design of baptism. The words are, " Baptize them into the name of the Father, and of the Son, and of the Holy Ghost." *Into*, not *in*, is the literal translation of the word which is obviously intended to explain the general design of baptism. The words in 1 Cor. xi. 24, "This do in remembrance of me," explain the design of the Lord's Supper. I naturally expect to find a similar statement of the design of baptism in the institution of that ordinance. Translate the words, *into the name of the Father, Son, and Holy Ghost*, and the expectation is answered. The disciple is baptized into the name, that is, into the faith, respecting the different persons of the Trinity. The ordinance is designed to represent the truth respecting the Trinity, that is, the saving truth, and all other revealed truth in connection with it, as actually received by the believer, together with his interest in all the blessed consequences of his faith. It is taken for granted that the person baptized believes the Gospel. Baptism is the profession of his faith, his hope in the promises made to believers, the ground of that hope, and his purpose of living according to the Gospel. I need hardly add, that the authority by which baptism is administered is implied. But the authority of the Trinity is not all that is intended by the words, for the words of the commission clearly intimate the design of the ordinance. The following Scriptures illustrate the same truth; Rom. vi. 3, 4 ; Gal. iii. 27 ; Col. ii. 12. Such is the general design of baptism. Allow me now to ask whether infants are capable of answering this design ? Need any be told that they are equally incapable of the perception and reception of the truth ? And, let me ask further, whether infants can be baptized when it must be allowed that they cannot answer the design of the ordinance ? Personal profession of the truth is essential to baptism. Where the truth is not professed there can be no baptism; for the very design of the ordinance is to represent the reception of the truth. This design of baptism is recognized by Pædo-baptists the most cautious and learned.

Let me ask, on what principle are infants excluded from the Lord's Supper, and the arguments for their admission repelled? The reply must be, Infants cannot answer the design of the Supper,—" Do this in remembrance of me ", and must therefore be excluded, notwithstanding their admission to the passover, and notwithstanding their admission, by many professing Christians, to the Lord's table. The reason for their rejection is valid, but not more so than the reason for refusing to baptize infants. The truth cannot be professed by them; they cannot answer the design of the ordinance. The presumption, therefore, remains valid; the design of baptism precludes the baptism of infants.

If we pass from the general design of baptism and attend to particulars, the truth will be still more apparent. Various examples shall be produced; at present I select regeneration.

XIII. A presumption against infant baptism arises from THE IMPOSSIBILITY OF ASCERTAINING THE REGENERATION OF INFANTS. One special design of baptism is to represent the regeneration of the baptized: Titus iii. 5; Eph. v. 26. Baptized infants are not all regenerated, for multitudes grow up and live and die in impenitence. Final impenitence is inconsistent with regeneration. Wherever the good work is begun, there God will perfect it till the day of Christ. Whether baptized or not, the finally impenitent were never regenerated. In the case of infants it is impossible to ascertain who are and who are not regenerated. Thus the presumption against infant baptism appears. The ceremony declares that the baptized person is regenerated, but facts often prove that he is not regenerated. A falsehood has been exhibited; but the exhibition of falsehood can never be required by the God of truth. I know of nothing that can, with any show of reason, be advanced against this presumption.

It may be said that the unregenerated were circumcised by the command of God. It is true; but the fact proves that circumcision was never designed, like baptism, to represent the regeneration of its subjects. It may be said that hypocrites are baptized. It is answered, God commands men to be baptized on a credible profession of their faith; but God has nowhere commanded hypocrites to be baptized; on the contrary, their baptism is prohibited. Had a command been given to baptize hypocrites, it would signify that hypocrites are regenerated, which is absurd. Were it commanded to baptize infants, the ordinance would indicate that baptized infants were regenerated, which is contrary to fact. Such suppositions could not possibly be regarded as facts without an impeachment of the Divine wisdom, truth, and consistency. It is therefore as certain that infants cannot be baptized as it is certain that God has appointed baptism to represent the regeneration of the baptized.

XIV. Another presumption against infant baptism arises from THE UNITY OF CHRISTIAN BAPTISM. The Scriptures speak of one baptism exclusively. "There is one body, and one Spirit, even as ye are called in one hope of your calling; One Lord, one faith, one baptism, one God and Father of all": Eph. iv. 4. In the same sense in which there is but one Lord and one God, there is but one baptism. Such is the doctrine of Scripture as to the unity of this ordinance. Admit, however, infant baptism, and we have more baptisms than one.

Infant baptism, supposing it to be an ordinance, would be an ordinance totally different from the baptism of the adult believer. Believer-baptism requires duties, antecedent, concomitant, and consequent to the ordinance: infant sprinkling rejects all duties, for infants can perform none. In believer-baptism (excepting our union with Christ and its consequences) there is nothing relative: in infant sprinkling everything is relative, nothing is personal. Believer-baptism, in all ordinary cases, is connected with the communion of saints; infant sprinkling in consistency requires it, but in fact rejects it. Believer-baptism is a symbol happily expressive of the great truths which baptism is designed to exhibit: infant baptism is, as to the design of baptism, totally unmeaning. In one word, these two operations agree in nothing except that the element of water is used in both. Believer-baptism is undeniably spoken of in the word of God, and therefore it is plain that infant baptism would be another and second initiatory ordinance. It is plain that the Scriptures recognise one baptism, exclusive of every other, for there is "one faith, one baptism, one God and Father of all"; hence it clearly follows that infant baptism is a human invention, and it is not one of the ordinances of Christianity.

Before concluding the presumptions against infant sprinkling, it may be useful to notice, that Christ's ordinances must be observed. Whether I have been sprinkled in infancy or not, it is my duty to be immersed after I have believed. If Christ has ordained an institution, it must be observed, because Christ has ordained it; and as the manner of observing the institution, as well as the institution itself, is of God, it must not only be observed, but observed likewise in the manner prescribed. "Now I praise you, brethren, that ye remember me in all things, and keep the ordinances, as I delivered them to you": 1 Cor. xi. 2. "Therefore, brethren, stand fast, and hold the traditions which ye have been taught, whether by word or our epistle": 2 Thess. ii. 15. Believer-baptism is one of these ordinances, and therefore must be observed. Were it not for infant sprinkling this would not be questioned. But the obligation to obedience remains, whatever may be the errors of men, and infant sprinkling cannot supersede it. This assertion will perhaps be denied. Many assign their having been sprinkled in infancy as their reason for not attending to baptism after believing. The reason, however, is not valid. Though I have been sprinkled in infancy, it is my duty, on believing, to be immersed. This assertion is interesting to not a few, and the history of the Acts of the Apostles puts its truth beyond a doubt. The Apostles baptized every adult convert, whether Jew or Gentile. Now, supposing circumcision to be baptism, and baptism circumcision, or, in other words, that the one comes in place of the other, every Jewish convert was twice baptized; his circumcision-baptism did not supersede his believer-baptism. The case must be the same still. If infant sprinkling came in the room of circumcision, the man sprinkled in infancy is in the same condition as the man circumcised in infancy. If the one were baptized after believing, so must the other be. Believer-baptism is no more superseded by infant sprinkling than it was by infant circumcision.

Leave, however, these groundless suppositions, and all uncertainty vanishes. Infant sprinkling is not revealed: believer-baptism is plainly revealed.

The question is practical. Am I to neglect what is incontestibly my duty on account of what cannot be proved to be a duty at all?

Thus, whether infant sprinkling succeed to circumcision or not, it cannot supersede baptism after believing.

LECTURE XII.

THE BAPTISM OF JOHN; ITS SUBJECTS AND MODE.

The reader will do well to compare and study Matt. iii.; Mark i. 1—11; xi. 30—33; Luke iii. 1—22; vii. 29—30; John i. 19—34; iii. 23; iv. 1; x. 40; Acts i. 5; xix. 1-7.

In discussing the subject of John's baptism we remark first upon ITS SUBJECTS.

1. *The subjects of John's baptism were adults.* Matt. iii. 5, 6: "Then went out to him Jerusalem, and all Judæa, and all the region round about Jordan, and were baptized of him in Jordan, confessing their sins." Verse 11 : "I indeed baptize you with water unto repentance," &c. Mark i. 4, 5 : " John did baptize in the wilderness, and preach the baptism of repentance for the remission of sins. And there went out unto him all the land of Judæa, and they of Jerusalem, and were all baptized of him in the river of Jordan, confessing their sins." Luke iii. 3: "And he (John) came into all the country about Jordan, preaching the baptism of repentance for the remission of sins." Verses 7, 8 : " Then said he to the multitude that came forth to be baptized of him . . . Bring forth therefore fruits worthy of repentance." Verses 21, 22 : "Now when all the people were baptized,

it came to pass, that Jesus also being baptized, and praying, the heaven was opened, and the Holy Ghost descended in a bodily shape like a dove upon him, and a voice came from heaven, which said, Thou art my beloved Son; in thee I am well pleased." John iv. 1 : " When therefore the Lord knew how the Pharisees had heard that Jesus made and baptized more disciples than John."

These last words show that both our Lord and the Baptist, his forerunner, baptized adults. Both made disciples, and then baptized them. They made disciples; that is, they instructed the applicants for baptism, and after these applicants were instructed they baptized them. Jesus himself began to be about thirty years of age when he was baptized. All the other scriptures respecting John's baptism prove that the subjects of John's baptism were adults.

2. *We find no account of the baptism or sprinkling of infants in any part of the record of John's ministry.* From the complexion of the narrative we are led to believe that infants were not baptized by John. " Then went out to him Jerusalem, and all Judæa, and all the region round about Jordan, and were baptized of him in Jordan, confessing their sins ": Matt. iii. 5, 6. This event is recorded by all the Evangelists; each of them amplifies the description. Their object required, and this amplification particularly required, the mention of children, had children been brought to John's baptism, or been baptized by him. To such as went out to him, John preached the baptism of repentance for the remission of sins. This circumstance is likewise repeatedly recorded. From this service infants

are excluded; they could not profit by the Baptist's preaching. Again such as were baptized by him are repeatedly said to confess their sins. Infants cannot confess sin. Once more, the Evangelist John tells us how baptism was administered both by Christ and his forerunner: John iv. 1. Thus, from the tenor of the narrative, we are led to believe that infants were not baptized by John.

3. *Qualifications incompetent to infants were required of such as were baptized by John.* Of this description is *repentance.* John preached the baptism of repentance for the remission of sins; he urged his hearers to bring forth fruits meet for repentance; and such as were baptized of him were baptized in Jordan, confessing their sins. I need not remark that infants are incapable of this qualification. *Faith in Christ* is another of the qualifications for baptism as administered by John. "Then, said Paul, John verily baptized with the baptism of repentance, saying unto the people that they should believe on him which should come after him, that is, on Christ Jesus": Acts xix. 4. There is no exception in favour of infants. A third qualification is *knowledge.* John preached to the candidates for his baptism, and by his preaching made disciples of them previous to baptism: Mark i. 4; John iv. 1. Infants cannot be made disciples in this way.

4. *Duties for which infants are incompetent were enjoined upon such as were baptized by John.*— Summary as is the account of the Baptist's labours, yet from it we learn the duties of the baptized. Previous to baptism a confession of sin was made. After baptism John exhorted his hearers to bring

forth fruits meet for repentance, or, as it is in the margin, answerable to amendment of life. It is evident that none of these duties could be performed by infants.

5. *The privileges of the baptized, as represented in the history of John's baptism, are remission of sins and its consequences.* Mark tells us, John did baptize in the wilderness, and preach the baptism of repentance for the remission of sins. It must be recollected that all the benefits of the covenant of grace are connected by an indissoluble tie; whoever, therefore, receives the remission of sins, receives along with it all the benefits of Christianity—grace, glory, and all subservient good. I make the remark, now, that the harmony between the baptism of John and the baptism of Christ may not be overlooked or mistaken. Infants cannot receive the symbol of these benefits, because they cannot give evidence that they believe.

6. *The design of the ordinance, according to the record of John's baptism, was to represent the truth which he preached as applied to his hearers.* He preached the same truth to all; but many rejected it, whilst many professed to receive it. These classes were distinguished by their submission to baptism, or by their rejecting it. "And all the people that heard him, and the publicans, justified God, being baptized with the baptism of John. But the Pharisees and lawyers rejected the counsel of God against themselves, being not baptized of him": Luke vii. 29, 30. Did John call them to repentance? By submitting to baptism they professed to repent. Did John say unto the people that they should believe on him which should come after

him, that is, on Christ Jesus? By submitting to his baptism they professed to believe that the kingdom was about to appear. Did John teach them to expect the remission of sins in this course? By submitting to baptism they professed their hope of this privilege. Did John teach them to bring forth fruits becoming repentance? By submitting to baptism they professed their purpose of acting accordingly. These things throw much light on a branch of this subject highly interesting, but apparently little understood. I need hardly add, that infants were incapable of answering this design, because they were unconscious of what was taking place.

7. Finally, *The principle on which infant sprinkling rests is rejected.* This principle is *descent*. Infants are generally sprinkled on the supposed grace of their parents, one or both, more immediate or more remote. But the plea of descent is expressly rejected in this history. "Think not to say within yourselves, We have Abraham to our father: for I say unto you, that God is able of these stones to raise up children unto Abraham. And now also the axe is laid unto the root of the trees; therefore every tree which bringeth not forth good fruit is hewn down, and cast into the fire": Matt. iii. 9, 10. This truth is repeated in the same connection and almost in the same words by the Evangelist Luke: the meaning is, that the evangelical differs from the legal dispensation. Though descent, under the law, entitled children to certain external privileges, under the Gospel it was unavailing. The religion of the Gospel is a thing altogether personal. The child cannot be baptized on the faith of his parent.

In further considering the baptism of John we are led next to consider ITS MODE.

The ordinance of baptism was corrupted, first, by admitting infants to baptism, instead of believers; and afterwards, by substituting sprinkling instead of immersion. We have adverted to the record of John's baptism, and we now come to examine the mode of baptism, as exhibited in that record. On examination we shall find all the satisfaction that can reasonably be desired, that John administered this ordinance by immersion.

1. Let us, first, attend to *the primary meaning of the word "baptize"*. The translators of the Bible have not translated this word at all, for what reason may easily be guessed. The word "immerse" would have condemned the general practice; the word "sprinkle" would not have given the sense of the word "baptize": they left it, therefore, as they found it in the original. The abettors of sprinkling have availed themselves of this circumstance, and tell us that though baptism is immersion, and although those who are immersed are rightly baptized, that yet to baptize may likewise signify to sprinkle; and, therefore, those who are sprinkled are rightly baptized, as well as those who are immersed. We must, therefore, assert first, what cannot be denied, that the first and primary meaning of the word "baptize", is to *immerse*. Of this the learned can satisfy themselves when they please by consulting their Greek lexicons; and the unlearned may satisfy themselves by desiring any scholar, on whose truth they can depend, to read to them from the dictionary

the first and natural meaning of the word "*baptize.*" *

Knowing the result, I shall hereafter take it for granted that the word "baptize" in the record means immerse. When John is said to baptize we are taught that he immersed.

2. You will recollect *the place where John administered the ordinance;* it was the river Jordan. Matt. iii. 5, 6: "Then went out to him Jerusalem, and all Judea, and all the region round about Jordan, and were baptized of him in Jordan." Ver. 13: "Then cometh Jesus from Galilee to Jordan unto John, to be baptized of him." Mark i. 5: "And there went out unto him all the land of Judea, and they of Jerusalem, and were all baptized of him in the river of Jordan." John x. 40: "And (Jesus) went away again beyond Jordan into the place were John at first baptized." Had John administered the ordinance by sprinkling, there was no necessity for putting himself and such multitudes out of Jerusalem and all Judea to the expense and trouble of repairing to the river Jordan. And I must add, had immersion been a matter of indifference, the Spirit of God would not have repeated so often what we have heard of the place where John baptized. This single consideration is sufficient to determine the practice of all who, like little children, learn the mind of Christ from the Scriptures. The Evangelist John has, however, in as many words, determined the matter. He tells us that much water was needed, and that

---

* See John xiii. 26; Luke xvi. 24; in both these passages the radical word signifies to dip or immerse.

this necessity determined the place of administration. "And John was baptizing in Ænon, near to Salim. because there was much water there; and they came and were baptized": John iii. 23. The enquirer will observe that the Holy Ghost has acquainted us with the reason why John baptized in Ænon— "there was much water there." If John administered the ordinance by immersion, the reason is good, but if by sprinkling, it is absurd. So plainly is the mode of baptism determined by the place selected by John for its administration.

3. *The prepositions* in, into, out, out of, *&c., prove that John administered the ordinance by immersion*. It is said of the multitude that they "were baptized of him *in* Jordan": Matt. iii. 6. We also read, "Jesus, when he was baptized, went up straightway *out of* the water; and, lo, the heavens were opened unto him, and he saw the Spirit of God descending like a dove, and lighting upon him: and lo a voice from heaven, saying, This is my beloved Son in whom I am well pleased": Matt. iii, 16, 17. It is natural to inquire, When was this voice heard? The answer is explicit: As soon as Christ went up *out of* the water. Suppose it had been translated, *from* the water, the time of this very interesting event would be left undetermined; we should not know whether it took place in the wilderness, or on the road; we should not know whether it took place on the day of the baptism, or on some other day. The correctness of the translation is ascertained both by the words and the circumstances. Christ's coming *up out of* the water, after baptism, shows that he went into the river Jordan, and was immersed there.

Mark i. 5—10. The inquirer will mark the similarity of language used by the different Evangelists, and the reason of it. In the whole record of John's baptism nothing whatever occurs in favour of sprinkling.

Whether we are bound to obey the Bible or not, I am not at present inquiring; that question has been fully discussed and determined. I take it for granted that we are bound to obey the Scriptures; and now, from the whole record, it appears that John administered the ordinance by immersion. To baptize is to immerse. Much water is necessary to immersion, but not to sprinkling. For the purpose of sprinkling it was worse than useless to go into a river. Add to all this, that immersion *is*, and sprinkling *is not*, a symbol significant of the design, duties, and privileges of the ordinance; and the conclusion is clear that baptism is immersion and nothing else.

LECTURE XIII.

BAPTISM OF THE DISCIPLES DURING CHRIST'S HUMILIATION. THE GREAT COMMISSION.

"After these things came Jesus and his disciples into the land of Judæa; and there he tarried with them, and baptized. And John also was baptizing in Ænon near to Salim, because there was much water there; and they came and were baptized. . . . And they came unto John, and said unto him, Rabbi, he that was with thee beyond Jordan, to whom thou barest witness, behold, the same baptizeth, and all men come to him. John answered and said, A man can receive nothing, except it be given him from heaven": John iii. 22, 23, 26, 27. "When, therefore, the Lord knew how the Pharisees had heard that Jesus made and baptized more disciples than John, (though Jesus himself baptized not, but his disciples), He left Judæa, and departed again into Galilee": John iv. 1—3.

Such is the record of the baptism by the disciples of Christ during his humiliation; but however summary, it leads to the same conclusions with the record of the baptism of John. To be satisfied of the justice of this remark, we must attend to the import of the words quoted, and the connection in which they stand.

1. As to the import of the words, we are told that *Christ made and baptized disciples.* To make disciples is, by teaching, to persuade men to be

further taught. Those who were made disciples were afterwards baptized. Such is the import of the words, and from them we learn the character of the subjects of Christ's baptism; they were neither infants nor ignorant, but taught, and capable of further teaching. They were first made disciples, and afterwards baptized.

2. As to the connection of the words, we find *the baptism of Christ and of John reported in one continuous narrative.* The narrative of Christ's baptism is continued in the same strain with the narrative of John's baptism: there is no hint that the character of the one is different from the character of the other; the inference is, that their leading character was the same. Suppose, that instead of Christ's baptism, an account of John's had been continued, it would be natural to infer that John continued to preach and baptize as before. The record of Christ's baptism must be explained on the same principle; we are bound to suppose that Christ's disciples taught and baptized in the same manner in which John taught and baptized. Some may need to be reminded that we are not now speaking of the disciples baptizing after the general commission, recorded in Matt. xxviii. and Mark xvi.; but of their baptizing previous to that commission. We call it Christ's baptism, because it was administered by his orders, during his humiliation. Previous to the general commission, we learn from the connection and strain of the words that Christ's disciples taught and baptized in the same manner as John. Observe, now, the consequence—all that we have heard of John's baptism must, for substance, be

applied to the baptism administered by the disciples of Christ. (1.) The design of John's baptism was to represent the application to his hearers of the truth which he preached, and which they professed to believe.* The design of Christ's baptism was the same; and as this design refers to professing disciples exclusively, so professing disciples

---

* The great object of John's baptism was the manifestation to Israel of the Son of God (John i. 31); and this manifestation was made by a figurative death, burial, and resurrection, shadowing forth what was afterwards to take place (1 Cor. xv. 3, 4.); and to this Jesus referred when he said, "I have a baptism to be baptized with": Luke xii. 50. He had been buried and raised in a figure at Jordan, but he was actually to descend into the lower parts of the earth that he might ascend up far above all heavens.

All the subjects of the kingdom which John was sent to announce were to have fellowship with the King in his death and resurrection (Col. ii. 12); for flesh and blood shall not inherit the kingdom of God. All, therefore, who professed repentance, and their readiness to receive Him whose coming John announced, were buried in Jordan, and raised again. When Jesus came to be baptized, John forbade him, for he knew the purity of his life and conversation (being his near kinsman), although he did not know he was the Messiah, till the voice from heaven, and the Holy Spirit resting upon him in the form of a dove,* made known his peerless dignity. That baptism was entirely new in Israel is evident from the question, why John baptized, if he were not Elias or the prophet? (Deut. xviii. 15.) During the Jewish Dispensation the precepts of Moses were neither to be increased nor diminished. If John were Elias or the prophet, he might, they thought, introduce what had not been hitherto commanded, but not otherwise. He replied, he was the forerunner of Christ.—J. H.

* Archbishop Leighton asks why the Holy Spirit descended upon Jesus in the form of a dove, and upon the apostles in the form of fire; and replies, because in the disciples there was much to purify, but Jesus was without spot.

exclusively were baptized by both. (2.) The qualifications for John's baptism were knowledge, faith, and repentance. The qualifications for Christ's baptism were the same. Infants do not possess these qualifications. (3.) The duties connected with John's baptism were confession of sins, and fruits meet for repentance. The duties connected with Christ's baptism were the same. Infants can perform none of these duties. (4.) The privileges represented in John's baptism were remission of sins and its consequences. The privileges represented by Christ's baptism were similar. These privileges belong to believers exclusively; and consequently the symbol belongs only to such as profess to believe. (5.) The subjects of John's baptism were adults. The words of the historian and the connection in which they stand prove that the subjects of Christ's baptism were adults also. (6.) John administered the ordinance by immersion. The words and the connection in which they stand prove that the disciples administered the ordinance in the same way; they baptized, that is, they immersed the disciples whom they had made.

THE COMMISSION TO THE APOSTLES.

"And Jesus came and spake unto them saying, All power is given unto me in heaven and in earth. Go ye, therefore, and teach all nations, baptizing them in the name of the Father, and of the Son, and of the Holy Ghost, teaching them to observe all things whatsoever I have commanded you; and, lo, I am with you alway, even unto the end of the world. Amen." Matt. xxviii. 18—20. "And he said unto them, Go ye into all the world, and preach the Gospel to every creature. He that believeth and is baptized shall be saved, but he that believeth not shall be damned": Mark xvi. 15, 16. Compare Luke xxiv. 45—49; John xx. 21—23.

Such is the commission which Christ gave to the Apostles; let us now attend to its import.

1. Respecting *the perpetuity of baptism.* It is baptism with water of which the commission speaks: Acts x. 47. Peter teaches us that baptism with water is not superseded by the reception of the Holy Ghost. Cornelius and his friends were baptized with water because they had already received the Holy Ghost. That the ordinance of water baptism was to continue to the end of the world appears in various ways, particularly from the connection in which it stands. It stands connected with teaching, preaching, and believing. "Go, teach all nations, baptizing them, teaching them to observe all things whatsoever I have commanded you." "Go, preach the Gospel to every creature; he that believes and is baptized shall be saved." Teaching, preaching, and believing are permanent duties, and the connection of baptism with permanent duties proves its own permanency. When Christ promises to be with the Apostles always to the end of the world, he teaches us that the commission shall remain in force to the end of the world.

2. Observe the import of the commission in respect of *the design of baptism,* which is to represent the truth as applied to the baptized. The Gospel is to be preached, the Gospel is to be believed, and the believer is to be baptized, that his reception of the Gospel may be exhibited. The

same thing appears from the expression, "Baptizing them into the name of the Father, of the Son, and of the Holy Ghost." The *name* of the Father, Son, and Holy Ghost means what the Scriptures teach concerning the Father, Son, and Holy Ghost; and to be baptized in or into this truth is to represent its application to the baptized. This doctrine comprehends what we are to believe, what we are to expect, and what we have to do. The symbol represents the faith, the hope, the duty of the baptized, corresponding to whatever is revealed respecting the Father, the Son, and the Holy Ghost.

3. Observe the import of the commission respecting *the qualifications of the baptized*. These qualifications are knowledge, faith, and repentance. Knowledge is a necessary qualification: "Go ye, therefore, and teach all nations, baptizing them." Faith is a requisite qualification: "He that believeth and is baptized shall be saved." Repentance is a requisite qualification. Accordingly Peter said to his hearers, "Repent and be baptized every one of you."

4. Observe, the doctrine of the commission respecting *the privileges of the baptized*. These privileges, in general, comprehend all that the believer is taught to expect from the Father, the Son, and the Holy Ghost; particularly, his baptism represents to the believer that he is "dead, and that his life is hid with Christ in God." His baptism represents to the believer that he shall be saved: "He that believeth and is baptized shall be saved." His baptism represents to the believer the remission of his sins. Hence Ananias said to Saul, "And

now, why tarriest thou? Arise and be baptized, and wash away thy sins"; and Peter tells us that baptism saves us, through the resurrection of Jesus Christ.

5. Observe the import of the commission in respect of *the duties connected with baptism*. These are all the duties connected with our holy religion. Previous to baptism we are bound to believe and profess our faith. The administrator must have evidence of that belief. Hence the words of Philip to the Ethiopian, "If thou believest with all thine heart, thou mayest" be baptized. During the administration, the baptized are bound to meet the truth represented in the ordinance with corresponding regard. "Baptism does also now save us (not the putting away of the filth of the flesh, but the answer of a good conscience toward God), by the resurrection of Jesus Christ." After baptism the believer is bound to justify his profession by his daily conduct. Hence these words in the commission, "teaching them to observe all things whatsoever I have commanded you".

6. Observe the import of the commission in respect of *the subjects of baptism*. These are believers: "He that believeth and is baptized shall be saved". Every man who hears the Gospel is bound to believe it; and everyone who believes it is bound to profess it, by being baptized; and everyone who is baptized is bound to observe all things whatsoever Christ has commanded. If there be any exception to this rule, the exception must be produced; if it cannot be produced, it becomes the duty of every one after believing to be baptized. This part of the commission calls for

the most serious attention of every man of principle.

7. Observe *the bearing of the commission on infant baptism.* We have just seen that the commission respects adults exclusively. Infants are as incapable of answering the design of baptism, as they are of answering the design of the Supper. Infants cannot exhibit the requisite qualifications of knowledge, faith, and repentance. The wicked lives of many who survive the age of infancy, prove that all infants, even the infants of believers, have no right to the privileges represented in baptism. Infants cannot perform the duties connected with baptism. The consequence is, they ought not to be baptized. The commission cannot be altered. It is not a little surprising, that a conclusion so plain should be resisted by reference to abrogated institutions, or to the plainly predicted corruptions of Christianity.

8. Observe the import of the commission in respect of *the mode of administering this ordinance.* The mode of administration is intimated, (1.) By the word *baptize,* which signifies to immerse. (2.) The symbol of immersion in water is very significant. We are reminded by the disciple of Christ being immersed in the name of the Trinity, that he is a mere recipient, and that salvation from first to last is altogether of the mercy and grace of God; we are reminded of his translation out of the kingdom of Satan into the kingdom of Christ; of his being brought out of the world into the church. Particularly, we see represented the death, burial, and resurrection of Christ, and our union with him in each of these. Hence the apostle says, "Know

ye not, that so many of us as were baptized into Jesus Christ were baptized into his death? Therefore we are buried with him by baptism into death: that like as Christ was raised up from the dead by the glory of the Father, even so we also should walk in newness of life": Rom. vi. 3, 4. The consequences of union with Christ are represented. We are by nature guilty, but our guilt is washed away in the blood of Christ. We are by nature corrupt; but we are sanctified, purified, or washed by the Spirit of Christ. We are by nature miserable; but we are refreshed by the Holy Spirit. Total immersion is peculiarly significant of that entire subjection by which genuine religion is distinguished. As the disciple of Christ goes into the water, he goes into Christianity, without reserve; he is immersed *into the name;* that is, into whatever is revealed respecting the Father, the Son, and the Holy Ghost; he goes into the truth as to faith, hope, and practice; with Christ he dies, and is buried; he becomes dead to sin through the death of Christ. He emerges out of the water; he rises with Christ to newness of life, and to share in all the consequences of his Saviour's resurrection. He puts off the old man, and puts on the new; he unites with the church, and there with his fellow-Christians, learns to observe all things whatsoever Christ has commanded him; and with them he enjoys the presence of his Lord.

I need hardly observe, that little or nothing of all this is exhibited in the baptism of an unconscious infant.

LECTURE XIV.

BAPTISM AT PENTECOST.

" And there were dwelling at Jerusalem Jews, devout men, out of every nation under heaven, (Parthians, Medes, &c.)— Ye men of Israel, hear these words; Jesus of Nazareth, a man approved of God among you by miracles, and wonders, and signs, which God did by him in the midst of you, as ye yourselves also know : Him, being delivered by the determinate counsel and foreknowledge of God, ye have taken, and by wicked hands, have crucified and slain : whom God hath raised up, having loosed the pains of death; because it was not possible that he should be holden of it.—This Jesus hath God raised up, whereof we all are witnesses. Therefore being by the right hand of God exalted, and having received of the Father the promise of the Holy Ghost, he hath shed forth this, which ye now see and hear.—Therefore let all the house of Israel know assuredly, that God hath made that same Jesus, whom ye have crucified, both Lord and Christ. Now when they heard this, they were pricked in their heart, and said unto Peter and to the rest of the apostles, Men and brethren, what shall we do ? Then Peter said unto them, Repent, and be baptized every one of you in the name of Jesus Christ, for the remission of sins, and ye shall receive the gift of the Holy Ghost. For the promise is unto you and to your children, and to all that are afar off, even as many as the Lord our God shall call. And with many other words did he testify and exhort, saying, Save yourselves from this untoward generation. Then they that gladly received his word were baptized : and the same day there were added unto them about three thousand souls ".—Acts ii. 5, 22, 23, 24, 32, 33, 36—41.

Such is the record of the first example of the manner in which the apostles executed the commission which they had received from their Lord. Let us now attend to its import.

1. The example harmonizes with the commission on *the perpetuity of baptism*. There is nothing in the narrative suggesting the temporary character of baptism. On the contrary, the question proposed by the Jews and answered by Peter is common to all convinced sinners in every age. Every mouth is stopped: the whole world is become guilty before God. Every one must put the question, What shall I do to be saved? And to every convinced sinner we must answer with Peter, "Repent, and be baptized every one of you in the name of Jesus Christ, and ye shall receive the gift of the Holy Ghost". The more particularly the answer is examined, the more clearly is the perpetuity of the ordinance evinced. The promise is not to be restricted to the Jews who first believed, but must be extended to their descendants to the end of time. "The promise is to you, and to your children". The promise is not to be limited to the Jews, or to the descendants of Jews, it must to the end of time be extended to all that are afar off, to every Jew and Gentile whom God shall call. "Make disciples, baptize and teach, and lo, I am with you alway, even to the end of the world".

2. The example harmonizes with the commission as to *the design of baptism*. There is a small difference in the preposition rendered *in*. In the commission, the preposition rendered *in* signifies *to*, or *into*. In the example, a different preposition

is used. The translators have rendered it *in* also; but, literally, it signifies *on*. Both, however, express the application of the truth to the mind. The English reader will, without the original, observe that *in the name*, here, though it implies, does not, in the first instance, signify, *by the command of*. When Peter directs them to be baptized in the name of Jesus Christ, he means that by their baptism they must signify that their minds have fixed *on* the doctrine respecting Jesus Christ. There is a small difference, also, in the adjunct to the word name. In the commission it is,—into the name of the Father, of the Son, and of the Holy Ghost. In the example it is,—upon the name of Jesus Christ. But the name of Jesus Christ is the Gospel; and the name of the Trinity is the same Gospel.

Thus, from the words of the commission, and from the example, we learn that the design of baptism is to represent the effectual application of the truth to the mind of the baptized. The matter leads to the same conclusion as the words. Peter charged his hearers with guilt. The truth took effect; they were pricked in their heart. Peter told them that the miracle which they witnessed was the seal of God appended to the apostles' commission. They believed him; they acknowledged him and his colleagues as ambassadors of God. Hence, they said unto Peter and to the rest of the apostles, Men and brethren, what shall we do? Peter preached to them the glad tidings of salvation through Christ. They gladly received his word; and of this effectual application of the truth to their minds baptism was the symbol.

3. The commission and the example are in harmony as to *the qualifications of the baptized*. According to the commission, the apostles were commanded to teach, to preach the Gospel. Peter and his colleagues faithfully executed their commission. To men out of every nation under heaven Peter preached or proclaimed the name of Christ, the truth concerning Christ; in particular, he preached repentance and the remission of sins. The qualifications of the baptized must correspond to this preaching. These qualifications are knowledge, faith, and repentance. The description of Peter's hearers exemplifies these qualifications.

4. The commission and the example harmonize as to *the privileges of the baptized*. The privileges of the baptized specified in the commission are salvation and the remission of sins. The specification in the example is of the same import, namely, the remission of sins and the gift of the Holy Ghost. The first Christians, when necessary, received and exercised the miraculous gifts of the Holy Ghost. These have ceased. The promise does not mean that they should continue, or even that all the first Christians possessed them. The promise refers especially to the Holy Ghost as the common privilege of all believers. If any man have not the Spirit of Christ, he is none of his. This is salvation. It is through the Spirit that the salvation of Christ is received.

The remission of sins, the other privilege specified by Peter, leads to the same hope. The remission of sins is, by an indissoluble tie, connected with salvation in all its parts. Rom. viii. 30. The privileges of the baptized, though differently expressed in the commission and the example, are the same for substance in both.

5. *The duties connected with baptism* are the same in the commission and the example. Those baptized at Pentecost, previous to their baptism professed their faith, otherwise the apostles could not have known who did, and who did not, gladly receive their word. Of their duties after baptism we have a very particular and interesting account in Acts ii. 41—47: " Then they that gladly received his (Peter's) word were baptized; and the same day there were added unto them about three thousand souls. And they continued stedfastly in the apostles' doctrine and fellowship, and in breaking of bread, and in prayers. And all that believed were together, and had all things common; and sold their possessions and goods, and parted them to all men, as every man had need. And they, continuing daily with one accord in the temple, and breaking bread from house to house, did eat their meat with gladness, and singleness of heart, praising God, and having favour with all the people. And the Lord added to the Church daily such as should be saved ". These words need no exposition. Those who gladly received Peter's word were baptized, were added to the Church immediately on their baptism, and attended, without exception, to the duties of their ecclesiastical relationship.

6. *The subjects baptized* are the same in the commission and in the example. In the commission the subjects of baptism are described as capable of attending to and believing the Gospel. They are commanded, after their baptism, to observe all things whatsoever Christ has required of them. In the

example this teaching and obedience are exhibited. The example on Pentecost certifies the import of the commission, as recorded by Matthew. Thus, from the execution of the commission by the inspired apostles we learn its unquestionable meaning. It has been quaintly said, that if infants be not in the apostles' commission, they are out of it: meaning, that if infants are not included, they must be excluded, for the commission cannot be altered.

Infant baptism or sprinkling has been supposed to be countenanced by these words in the narrative, "For the promise is unto you and to your children." But the supposition is unfounded. That the word *children* does not in this place signify infants, but adult descendants, appears from two considerations. (1.) The prophet, quoted by Peter, speaks of the sons and daughters of the children of Israel as capable of prophesying; that is, as adult: Acts ii. 16—18. " But this is that which was spoken by the prophet Joel: and it shall come to pass in the last days, saith God, I will pour out of my Spirit upon all flesh; and your sons and your daughters shall prophesy, and your young men shall see visions, and your old men shall dream dreams: and on my servants and on my handmaidens I will pour out in those days of my Spirit, and they shall prophesy". The promise, in the words of the prophet, is this—" I will pour out of my Spirit upon all flesh, and your sons and your daughters shall prophesy". The words of Peter are, " Repent, and be baptized every one of you, in the name of Jesus Christ, and ye shall receive the gift of the Holy Ghost; for the promise (of the Holy Ghost) is (by the prophet Joel, made) unto you, and to your children";—you, your sons and your daughters, shall prophesy. Those whom Peter calls children, therefore, the prophet calls sons and daughters, capable of prophesying.

It has been alleged that by the promise here we are to understand the general promise of the Messiah, and not the particular promise of the Holy Ghost. But this is alleged without proof; and not only without proof, but in the face of very decisive evidence to the contrary. Let the inquirer compare the prophecy, Joel, chap. ii., with the quotation and application of it, in Acts ii., and he will, without assistance, perceive that what Peter calls the promise, is the promise of the Spirit, as given by the prophet. He will observe, that the apostle expressly quotes the prophet Joel as predicting the effusion of the Holy Ghost which they witnessed: verse 16, "For *this* is that which was spoken by the prophet Joel". And the inquirer will observe that Peter tells his hearers, that they themselves, as well as the apostles, might receive the Holy Ghost. "Repent, and be baptized every one of you, in the name of Jesus Christ, and ye shall receive the Holy Ghost". He proves his assertion from the prophet. The promise is not to us apostles only, but to all flesh, particularly to you and to your children; your sons and your daughters shall prophesy.

The inquirer will observe, further, how the promise concludes in Joel, and how that conclusion is quoted by the apostle. The concluding words of the prophet are these: "And it shall come to pass, that whosoever shall call on the name of the Lord shall be delivered: for in Mount Zion and in Jerusalem shall be deliverance, as the Lord hath said, and in the remnant whom the Lord shall call": Joel ii. 32. The words of Peter are in verses 21 and 22. "And it shall come to pass, that whosoever shall call on the name of the Lord shall be saved. Ye men of Israel, hear these words". And after proving from Ps. xvi. the death and resurrection of Christ, he adds in verses 38 and 39, "Repent, and be baptized every one of you, in the name of Jesus Christ, for the remission of sins, and ye shall receive the gift of the Holy Ghost; for the promise (quoted from Joel), is unto you, and to your children (your sons and daughters), and to all that are afar off, even as many as the Lord our God *shall call*".

"The remnant" means the Israelites remaining after their captivity, whether near Jerusalem or far off from it, and also the Gentiles (all flesh), even as many as the Lord our God shall call: "the remnant whom the Lord shall call". So evident is it, that the prophecy of Joel respecting the Holy Ghost and salvation is the promise of remission of sins, and the Holy Ghost, mentioned by Peter. But, (2.) Independently of the prophecy, it is certain, from the words of Peter himself, that by children he means adult descendants. These children, to whom the promise is made, are twice described: "And it shall come to pass, that whosoever shall call on the name of the Lord shall be saved." And they are again described as those "whom the Lord should call": verses 21, 39. Infants may be sanctified, but they cannot be called: calling supposes that the Gospel is preached and heard: effectual calling supposes that the Gospel is preached, heard, and obeyed.

Having sufficiently exposed the vulgar perversion of this Scripture, I am at liberty to observe, that, in so far as this example is concerned, infant baptism must be rejected.

7. The commission and the example agree in *the mode of baptism*. In the history of the example we have these words: "And the same day there were added unto them about three thousand souls." This fact is supposed to be inconsistent with immersion. Where, it is asked, was there water sufficient for immersing three thousand? And supposing that water is found, it is asked further, how twelve men could, during the part of the day that remained after Peter's sermon, examine, baptize, and admit to the church a number so great? But the answer is easy. An inspired record must be credited, though we cannot explain the things recorded. Besides, the words of the history do not require us to believe that the three thousand were baptized on *the day* of their conversion. The words are, "Then they that gladly received his word were baptized". Neither does the historian say, that all the converts were baptized by the apostles *in person*. The other disciples, as in the case of Cornelius, might share the labour with the apostles. As to water, there was abundance in and about Jerusalem. But whether we can or cannot explain it, we have full assurance of the fact. The historian tells us that they that gladly received the apostle's word were baptized; that is, they were immersed.

Should it be asked, whether we are obliged to understand the word "*baptize*" in the sense of immersion? I answer, assuredly we are, for the following reasons: (1.) Immerse is the natural and primary meaning 'of the word baptize. (2.) We must understand the word in the same sense in which the same writer uses it elsewhere. In his history of the baptism of the Ethiopian eunuch, the word, beyond all reasonable doubt, is used in the sense of immersion: Acts viii. 36. The New Testament has but one Author. The Holy Spirit dictated the whole, though he employed different amanuenses. When any author explains his own words, according to that explanation we must understand them, when used without explanation. By three of the evangelists, in the history of John's baptism, we have seen that the Spirit uses the word baptize in the sense of immersion. How, then, are we to understand him when using the pen of the other evangelist? In the same sense, assuredly, in which he uses it when explained. This, we have seen, is immersion; therefore, in the record before us we must understand it in the sense of immersion also.

The more learned abettors of sprinkling, aware of the primary meaning of the word "baptize", and that the Holy Spirit uses it in the sense of immersion, have strained every nerve to show that, in some instances, the word is used in the New Testament in the sense of sprinkling. They have quoted the baptism of the Holy Ghost, the divers washings mentioned in the Hebrews, and particularly Mark vii. 3, 4. But to no purpose. The primary meaning of words in a plain narrative is not to be learned from figures of speech. It has never yet been proved that the word baptize is used in the sense of sprinkling. Suppositions prove nothing. As to Mark, the words are, "For the Pharisees, and all the Jews, except they wash their hands oft, eat not, holding the tradition of the elders. And when they come from the market, except they wash, they eat not. And many other things there be which they have received to hold, as the washing of cups, and pots, brazen vessels, and of tables"—in the margin it is *beds*. The word rendered *wash*, is, in the original, baptize, and how can these pieces of furniture be immersed? But the question recurs, and to what end should they be sprinkled? We are not acquainted with the nature of the articles specified; whatever they were, the historian tells us that they were purified by immersion; and what an inspired writer tells us, it is our duty to believe, whether we can explain the matter recorded or not.

I shall conclude this lecture by remarking, that the illustrious example, which is furnished us by the great ingathering of Pentecost, is a pattern in all the concerns of baptism, to be imitated by all churches in all ages. I have, therefore, particularly marked its various details, and in each of them pointed out the harmony of the example with the commission. It has been fully proved that the Acts of the Apostles are recorded for the regulation of the churches. The conclusion is plain—this pattern must be imitated. By it, in connection with the commission and other examples, we must regulate our judgment and practice as to the perpetuity, design, qualifications, privileges, duties, subjects, and mode of this ordinance.

LECTURE XV.

BAPTISM OF THE SAMARITANS AND OF THE ETHIOPIAN EUNUCH.

"Then Philip went down to the city of Samaria, and preached Christ unto them. And the people with one accord gave heed unto those things which Philip spake, hearing and seeing the miracles which he did. For unclean spirits, crying with loud voice, came out of many that were possessed with them: and many taken with palsies, and that were lame, were healed. And there was great joy in that city. But there was a certain man, called Simon, which beforetime in the same city used sorcery, and bewitched the people of Samaria, giving out that himself was some great one: to whom they all gave heed, from the least to the greatest, saying, This man is the great power of God. And to him they had regard, because that of long time he had bewitched them with sorceries. But when they believed Philip preaching the things concerning the kingdom of God, and the name of Jesus Christ, they were baptized, both men and women. Then Simon himself believed also; and when he was baptized, he continued with Philip, and wondered, beholding the miracles and signs which were done. Now when the apostles which were at Jerusalem heard that Samaria had received the word of God, they sent unto them Peter and John; who, when they were come down, prayed for them that they might receive the Holy Ghost: (for as yet he was fallen upon none of them: only they were baptized in the name of the Lord Jesus.) Then laid they their hands on them, and they received the Holy Ghost. And when Simon saw that through laying on of the apostles' hands the Holy Ghost was given, he offered them money, saying, Give me also this power, that on whomsoever I lay hands, he may receive the Holy Ghost. But Peter said unto him, Thy money perish with thee, because thou hast thought that the gift of God may be purchased with money. Thou hast neither part nor lot in this matter: for thy heart is not right in the sight of God. Repent therefore of this thy wickedness, and pray God, if perhaps the thought of thine heart may be forgiven thee. For I perceive that thou art in the gall of bitterness, and in the bond of iniquity. Then answered Simon, and said, Pray ye to the Lord for me, that none of these things which ye have spoken come upon me ".—Acts viii. 5—24.

1. The commission of our Lord and the practice of the early church harmonize in this instance as in every other as to the design of baptism.

The design of the ordinance is to represent the personal application of the truth to the baptized. According to Matthew's gospel the apostles, in their commission, are commanded to begin with "teaching"; or as Mark has it, with "preaching." This was done at Samaria, for Philip went down to the city and preached Christ unto them. The matter to be preached is the name of the Father, Son, and Holy Ghost—the Gospel of repentance and remission of sins, according to the commission. Philip preaches the same things, for we read that he preached "concerning the kingdom and the name of Jesus Christ." The apostles, in the commission, are next commanded to baptize the disciples *into* the name of the Father, Son, and Holy Ghost. In obedience to the same commission, Philip baptizes the believing Samaritans *in*—literally, *to* or *into*— the name of the Lord Jesus. The preposition here is the same as in the commission. Both the preposition and the adjunct lead to the same conclusion as to the design of baptism, which is to represent the personal application of the truth to the baptized.

2. The qualifications for baptism are the same in the commission and in the example at Samaria, namely, knowledge, faith, and repentance. They had *knowledge,* for " the people with one accord gave heed unto those things which Philip spake " : verse 6. They heard, and understood and rejoiced in that which Philip preached respecting Christ. The Samaritans had *faith.* Verse 12 : " But when they believed Philip preaching the things concerning the kingdom of God, and the name of Jesus Christ, they were baptized ". Verse 13 : " Then Simon himself believed also ". We are particularly acquainted with the evidence on which they believed ; verses 6, 7 : " And the people with one accord gave heed unto those things which Philip spake, hearing and seeing the miracles which he did. For unclean spirits, crying with loud voice, came out of many that were possessed with them : and many taken with palsies, and that were lame, were healed ". Their *repentance* is intimated in their turning from Simon to Philip ; verses 10—12.

3. The example before us is in harmony with the commission as to the privileges and duties connected with baptism. The privileges comprehend salvation; and the duties comprehend whatever Christ has commanded : both are implied in the Samaritans being baptized in the name of Christ. The name of Christ means everything said in the Scriptures concerning him. It implies

all the promises that are made to believers, and all the duties that are required of them.

4. The example obliges us to reject the practice of pædo-baptism and sprinkling. Without precept or pattern nothing can be observed as an ordinance of Christ. If the subjects of baptism are to be determined by the persons baptized in Samaria, infants must be excluded, for they are not mentioned in the record.

And how is this omission to be accounted for, if the infants of Samaritan believers were baptized? The omission is not to be accounted for from Luke's manner of writing. It is not his manner to omit the concerns of children : we may refer to Luke xviii. 15, and Acts xxi. 5. If infants were baptized in Samaria, and the historian has not mentioned the circumstance, he has altered his usual mode of writing. The omission cannot be accounted for on the supposition that it was a matter of small moment; the Baptist controversy proves the contrary, for in view of that discussion the mention of the infant baptism at Samaria would have been of great value. The baptism of the Samaritan infants, if they had been baptized, would, without doubt, have been a matter of unspeakably greater moment than Christ's touching infants, or children accompanying Paul to his ship: since, then, Luke has mentioned the less he would also have mentioned the greater had it occurred. The omission cannot be accounted for on the supposition of the prevalence of the practice of infant baptism; for, however prevalent it may be supposed to have been, the practice of adult baptism must have been still more prevalent in the days of the apostles. On this supposition, we had never heard anything of baptism at all, since its prevalence would have been in other cases as well as this a reason for silence in reference to it. The omission cannot be accounted for on the principle that everything is not recorded in every place; because here, had infants been baptized, their baptism could not have been omitted, since the historian gives us a particular account of the persons baptized. They who believed and were baptized are stated to have been both *men* and *women;* if infants were baptized, the enumeration is incomplete. The omission cannot be accounted for on the supposition that the historian's design did not require the mention of infants. His design is intimated in the title of his work, "The Acts of the Apostles". Had infant baptism or sprinkling belonged to these acts, fidelity required its insertion. The omission cannot be accounted for on the supposition of oversight. Inspiration is, in every instance, inconsistent with error. Let the inquirer consider these things, and he will be convinced that the Holy Spirit directed Luke to a special enumeration, in order that, to the end of time, men might learn from his *silence* respecting infants as well as from his explicitness as to the baptism of *men and women.* The corruption of Christianity in the matter of Pædo-baptism was foreseen, and a significant caution against it was provided in the utter silence of inspired writers.

5. From this example, as from the commission, we learn that *men and women* after believing, are bound to be baptized. If, then, apostolical practice is a rule of duty, we ourselves, like the Samaritans, must, after believing, observe this ordinance.

6. The commission and this example are in harmony as to the mode of baptism. The language is the same in both. I hope it is unnecessary to repeat the remarks already made on the word *baptize*, either respecting its primary meaning, or use in the sacred writings; and as there is nothing peculiar in this instance, I shall proceed to the next. Allow me, however, previously to observe two things:—

1. That the whole Scripture, as far as we have advanced, speaks the same language, and leads to the same conclusion. The commission requires the baptism of believers exclusively. The apostles, first at Jerusalem, and next at Samaria, taught and baptized their converts, and they baptized none other.

2. On reducing these principles to practice, a distinction must be made between the sincerity and credibility of a Christian profession. This is vividly brought before us by the case of Simon, who is said to have believed and therefore was baptized, who nevertheless turned out to be in the gall of bitterness. Some of the abettors of impure communion have confounded these things, and by the confusion misled the unwary. You cannot judge the heart, say they, and therefore the pursuit of pure communion is illusory. The answer is easy. The churches pretend not to judge the heart; they can, however, judge the external conduct. Where the profession is belied by action, it cannot be admitted, though the professor may be a believer. On the contrary, where a profession is distinctly made, and not contradicted by practice, it ought to be admitted, though, in

the sight of God, the professor is not accepted, because, in fact, he does not believe. All this is illustrated and confirmed by the example before us. The profession of Simon was credible, and therefore rightly admitted by Philip; it was insincere, and therefore rejected by God. The fact is recorded as a warning to professors and a rule for the churches.

BAPTISM OF THE ETHIOPIAN EUNUCH.

"And the angel of the Lord spake unto Philip, saying, Arise, and go toward the south unto the way that goeth down from Jerusalem unto Gaza, which is desert. And he arose and went: and, behold, a man of Ethiopia, an eunuch of great authority under Candace queen of the Ethiopians, who had the charge of all her treasure, and had come to Jerusalem for to worship, was returning, and sitting in his chariot read Esaias the prophet. Then the Spirit said unto Philip, Go near, and join thyself to this chariot. And Philip ran thither to him, and heard him read the prophet Esaias, and said unto him, Understandest thou what thou readest? And he said, How can I, except some man should guide me? And he desired Philip that he would come up and sit with him. The place of the Scripture which he read was this, He was led as a sheep to the slaughter; and like a lamb dumb before his shearer, so opened he not his mouth: In his humiliation his judgment was taken away: and who shall declare his generation? for his life is taken from the earth. And the eunuch answered Philip, and said, I pray thee, of whom speaketh the prophet this? of himself, or of some other man? Then Philip opened his mouth, and began at the same scripture, and preached unto him Jesus. And as they went on their way, they came unto a certain water: and the eunuch said,

See, here is water: what doth hinder me to be baptized? And Philip said, If thou believest with all thine heart, thou mayest. And he answered and said, I believe that Jesus Christ is the Son of God. And he commanded the chariot to stand still; and they went down both into the water, both Philip and the eunuch; and he baptized him. And when they were come up out of the water, the Spirit of the Lord caught away Philip, that the eunuch saw him no more: and he went on his way rejoicing. But Philip was found at Azotus: and passing through, he preached in all the cities, till he came to Cæserea." Acts viii. 26—40.

This example teaches us nothing directly of the perpetuity or design of baptism, or of the privileges represented by it. On these things, therefore, I shall make only two summary remarks :—

1. Though nothing be directly taught of the design and privileges of baptism, yet, indirectly, we are taught the same doctrine as before. The design is implied in the transaction, and the privileges in Philip's doctrine respecting Jesus. The subject is of the same character as the subjects in the preceding examples. On the head of perpetuity, we have nothing opposed to the former evidence.

2. This and other examples of baptism recorded in the New Testament mutually explain and throw light on each other. Inattention to this principle of exposition has led to consequences very unhappy. The Scriptures (such as 1 Cor. chap. v.) often and imperiously require the exclusion of bad men from the churches; but because in some instances—such as the Asiatic churches—the command is not repeated, impure communion has been vindicated. The vindication is inadmissable. The character of the materials of churches must be learned from all

the Scriptures on the subject taken together. A disciplined Christian must apply the principle to every topic of inquiry, and every particular of practice; and, amongst the rest, to the subject of baptism. On the other branches of the baptist question, we have, in the example, additional information.

1. We are informed that faith is a qualification indispensable for this ordinance. Verse 37: "And Philip said, If thou believest with all thine heart, thou mayest" (be baptized). The translation is correct; but there is an emphasis in the word rendered "thou mayest", which ought to be noticed. Literally, it signifies, *it is permitted, it is lawful;* meaning, that if he did not believe with all his heart, it was not permitted, it was not lawful. There is a universality in the declaration which ought likewise to be noticed. It is not restricted to the Ethiopian; the declaration is general, it is allowed, it is lawful; meaning, that in no case would it be lawful without faith. This emphasis is confirmed by the connection. The Ethiopian had asked what hindered him to be baptized. Philip answers that nothing hindered him, if he believed; but that if he did not believe, there was an insurmountable hinderance, namely, the want of this qualification. It is implied that in every instance the want of faith would disqualify for baptism. Thus additional light is thrown on the commission which is seen to mean, "He that believes and is baptized shall be saved; but he that believes not, can neither be saved nor baptized".

2. We have additional information respecting one of the duties connected with baptism, namely, a profession of faith. A profession of faith previous

BAPTISM OF THE ETHIOPIAN EUNUCH. 179

to baptism is supposed in every example we have hitherto examined. That our exposition of the record in each of these instances has been correct, is fully confirmed by the history of the Ethiopian's baptism. In this example the matter is expressly stated: the evangelist requires, and the candidate for baptism gives, an explicit confession of faith. Further, the character of the baptismal confession is fully ascertained: "If thou believest with, from, or out of, *all thine heart*, thou mayest". If it be inquired, To what end does Philip say, "If thou believest with all thine heart, thou mayest"?—for answer let it be observed, that the expression, Jesus Christ is the Son of God, signifies amongst other things, that Jesus is a Prophet, Priest, and King. The Ethiopian says that he believes this. But does he believe in a theoretical, or a practical sense? Does he believe on him as the rulers, who did not confess him? Or does he intend to take his instructions from him as a Prophet,—to depend on his merits as a Priest,—to submit to him, and obey him as a King? Does he believe to practice? Does he believe with the heart? Philip's question includes the practical purposes of the man; and the Ethiopian's answer in this connection means that in a practical sense he believed that Jesus Christ was the Son of God. Thus we find that a Scriptural profession of the faith must comprehend both the theoretical opinions and the practical purposes of the persons to be baptized.

3. We have information as satisfactory as we could reasonably desire respecting the mode of baptism. The words are these, verse 36: "And as

they went on their way, they came unto a certain water: and the eunuch said, See, here is water; what doth hinder me to be baptized"? Verses 38, 39: "And he commanded the chariot to stand still: and they went down both into the water, both Philip and the eunuch; and he baptized him. And when they were come up out of the water, the Spirit of the Lord caught away Philip". The meaning of the words is plainly this: they came to a certain water; Philip and the Ethiopian went both down into the water; when both were in the water, Philip immersed the Ethiopian; and then both Philip and the Ethiopian came up out of the water. It has been objected, that, according to this argument, Philip was baptized as well as the eunuch. I answer, that this objection is founded either on a mistake, or a palpable misrepresentation of the argument. The argument does not suppose that going down into the water and being baptized are the same thing. It supposes that these are different, and that, after both Philip and the Ethiopian had gone down into the water, Philip immersed the Ethiopian. The argument proceeds on three points: (1.) That the primary meaning of the word baptize is to immerse; (2.) That the sacred writers use the word in the sense of immersion, without ever using it in any other sense; (3.) That the circumstances of the case lead us, in this example, to understand the word in the sense of immersion. What made Philip and the eunuch both go down into the water, unless the immersion of the eunuch had been necessary? It is highly probable, from the route by which they were travelling, that they had along with them a quantity of water

BAPTISM OF THE ETHIOPIAN EUNUCH. 181

sufficient for the purpose of sprinkling. They needed not, unless for immersion, to wait till they came to this water. Had sprinkling been all that was necessary, the servants, from the state observed in the East, would no doubt have handed up to Philip the water which he needed. If Philip must himself take up the water in the palm of his hand, what necessity was there for the Ethiopian wetting himself in the water? He might have been sprinkled in the chariot. But if both of them go down, why does Philip go *into* the *water?* He could, had not immersion been necessary, with more convenience to himself have administered sprinkling by the side of the water; and, lastly, if Philip must go into the water, what, excepting immersion, made it necessary for the eunuch to go into the water? The question is not to be evaded by saying that when the chariot came to the water they went down to the side of it, and again came up. The prepositions are changed, and each of them is emphatical. When the chariot is said to come *to* the water, the preposition used signifies *close upon;* when the chariot came *close upon* the water. When they *went down*, the preposition signifies *to* or *into;* but the translators have preferred *into*, and for good reason, because the next preposition implies that they were *in it;*—after the baptism they came both up *out of* the water. Connect with each of these remarks the fact, that the word baptize signifies to immerse. As to the objection, it is not said that Philip was immersed; it only said that Philip immersed the eunuch As to the evasion, Philip did not go from the water into the chariot, for as soon as they came out of the water, the Spirit of the Lord carried him away. So satisfactory, in every way, is the evidence that the Ethiopian was immersed.

4. According to this example, infant baptism must be rejected. According to it, knowledge, faith, and a profession of faith, are requisite to baptism. It need hardly be added, that these things are not found in infants.

5. The baptism of the Ethiopian is an example of baptism after believing, commanded, approved, and recorded by the Holy Ghost; and if infant sprinkling be a nullity, as assuredly it is, it becomes the duty of every man and woman, after believing, to be immersed. I conclude with noticing, what must be obvious to all, that the baptism of the Ethiopian eunuch is in perfect harmony with the apostle's commission, and with the other examples at Jerusalem and Samaria.

LECTURE XVI.

BAPTISM OF SAUL OF TARSUS, AND OF THE CENTURION.

"And there was a certain disciple at Damascus, named Ananias; and to him said the Lord in a vision, Ananias. And he said, Behold, I am here, Lord. And the Lord said unto him, Arise, and go into the street which is called Straight, and inquire in the house of Judas for one called Saul of Tarsus: for, behold, he prayeth, and hath seen in a vision a man named Ananias coming in, and putting his hand on him, that he might receive his sight. Then Ananias answered, Lord, I have heard by many of this man, how much evil he hath done to thy saints at Jerusalem: And here he hath authority from the chief priests to bind all that call on thy name. But the Lord said unto him, Go thy way: for he is a chosen vessel unto me, to bear my name before the Gentiles, and kings, and the children of Israel: For I will show him how great things he must suffer for my name's sake. And Ananias went his way, and entered into the house; and putting his hands on him, said, Brother Saul, the Lord, even Jesus, that appeared unto thee in the way as thou camest, hath sent me, that thou mightest receive thy sight, and be filled with the Holy Ghost. And immediately there fell from his eyes as it had been scales: and he received sight forthwith, and arose, and was baptized. And when he had received meat, he was strengthened. Then was Saul certain days with the disciples which were at Damascus. And straightway he preached Christ in the synagogues, that he is the Son of God. But all that heard him were amazed, and said; Is not this he that destroyed them which called on this name in Jerusalem, and came hither for that intent, that he might bring them bound unto the chief priests? But Saul increased the more in strength, and confounded the Jews which dwelt at Damascus, proving that this is very Christ ".—Acts ix. 10—22.

"And one Ananias, a devout man according to the law, having a good report of all the Jews which dwelt there, came unto me, and stood, and said unto me, Brother Saul, receive thy sight. And the same hour I looked up upon him. And he said, The God of our Fathers hath chosen thee, that thou shouldest know his will, and see that Just One, and shouldest hear the voice of his mouth. For thou shalt be his witness unto all men of what thou hast seen and heard. And now why tarriest thou? arise, and be baptized, and wash away thy sins, calling on the name of the Lord ".—Acts xxii. 12—16.

On the perpetuity and design of baptism, nothing occurs in this example inconsistent with the preceding examples, or with the commission. 1. The qualifications of knowledge, faith, and repentance are implied in the narrative. 2. Respecting the privileges connected with baptism we have something very specific. The privilege specified is the remission of sins. " Arise, and wash away thy sins ". As remission of sins is indissolubly connected with the other benefits of the covenant of grace, this is in harmony with the preceding example. But it is still more specific. I refer to the explicit application of the privilege to the person baptized. Baptism represents our guilt: washing supposes pollution. Baptism represents the atonement, the fountain opened for sin and for uncleanness. But it represents more, even the removal of the guilt of the individual baptized. This design of baptism is implied in the commission, and in every example hitherto considered. It is particularly noticed in the baptism at Pentecost; Acts ii. 38. The meaning in that place is the same with the words under consideration, but they are not so explicit. The words before us explicitly apply the privilege to Paul. "Arise, and wash away thy sins." This is the unquestionable meaning of Ananias's language, and it is a matter of consequence. It distinguishes baptism from circumcision. Circumcision was a seal of the righteousness of faith; but it was not a seal of the application of that righteousness to the individual circumcised. Hence, it was administered to unbelievers, infants, and such as were never saved; to Ishmael, Esau, and all the descendants of Abraham, whether believers or unbelievers. It was a seal of the covenant made with Abraham. It represented the certainty of Messiah's advent in his family; the salvation of such as imitated the faith of the patriarch; and the assurance of the other promises of that covenant. But, directly, it sealed nothing to the individual circumcised. From the example before us, we find that the design of baptism is different. The privilege is confirmed to the individual, provided the profession upon which he is baptized be sincere. Paul's sins were not washed away by the water of baptism, but the water of baptism represented the removal of *his* sins: "Arise, and be baptized, and wash away *thy* sins". It is of consequence to mark and rrcollect this fact. It proves that the subjects of baptism must be believers; for without faith there is no forgiveness. It proves that infants cannot be baptized; because they can give no evidence of faith, nor can they be bidden to wash away their sins. The words of Ananias cannot be applied to an infant. The difference between hypocrites and infants was formerly noticed, and need not be repeated here.

3. Two of the duties connected with baptism are here particularly specified—calling on the name of the Lord, and church-association.

So closely is the first of these duties connected with Christianity in general, that it is employed to designate its professors. Acts ix. 13, 14: "Then Ananias answered, Lord, I have heard by many of this man, how much evil he hath done to thy saints at Jerusalem: and here he hath authority from the chief priests to bind all that *call on thy name*". It is the Lord Jesus Christ whom Ananias is addressing. He designates Christians by their duty, "calling on the name of the Lord Jesus". It is to be expected that they who are baptized in the name of the Lord should call on that name. But we are not left to inference. Saul is expressly commanded to connect this duty with his baptism: "Arise, and be baptized, and wash away thy sins, calling on the name of the Lord".

There is no reason for restricting the performance of this duty to the time occupied in immersion, neither is there any reason for excluding it from that time. All for which we contend is, without doubt, implied in the form of expression made use of; I mean, that calling on the name of the Lord is a duty connected with baptism. There is a striking analogy between the forms of expression, "calling on the name of the Lord", and "discerning the Lord's body". Discerning the Lord's body is essential to the right observance of the ordinance of the Supper; and incapacity for discerning the Lord's body is sufficient to disqualify for that ordinance. The impartial inquirer will, in the case of baptism, draw the same conclusion from the same premises. Calling on the name of the Lord is essential to baptism, and incapacity for calling on the name of the Lord is a sufficient disqualification for that ordinance. The cases are parallel. Bodily service profits as little in the one case as in the other. If there be any difference, it is this :—in the case of the Supper the conclusion follows from the premises; but in the case of baptism it is expressly asserted that it follows : 1 Peter iii. 21.

The other duty mentioned—church-association, is likewise, though perhaps, not so particularly intimated. We have the words, Acts ix. 19, "And when he had received meat, he was strengthened. Then was Saul certain days with the disciples which were at Damascus". Saul is no sooner baptized than he connects himself with the church : qualified for baptism, he is qualified for church-association. It is in the face of consistency, and in the face of Scripture, that the abettors of sprinkling plead that infants are qualified for baptism, but not for church-communion in all its parts.

4. The bearing of Saul's baptism on the case of infants has been noticed. We have seen that the spirit of the record is against infant baptism. Allow me to remark, that by this and similar Scriptures, every conscientious inquirer must be determined.

These Scriptures shine in their own light. To attempt to explain them by Scriptures more obscure is worse than absurd; and worse still, to contradict them by imaginary inferences from abrogated institutions. So far as we have examined, not one vestige of infant sprinkling has appeared; on the contrary, the further we advance, the condemnatory evidence is multiplied and strengthened. Let us persevere in the investigation until we have examined every Scripture on the subject.

5. From the baptism of Saul we have additional evidence that every man, after believing, ought to be baptized. That Saul's is an example of believer-baptism needs no further illustration or proof. But does infant sprinkling absolve us from the duty of imitating the example? The nature of the ceremony, and the history of Paul, oblige us to answer in the negative. He tells us himself that he was a Hebrew of the Hebrews, and circumcised the eighth day, in consequence of his descent. It has been proved that baptism is neither circumcision nor a substitute for it. But, suppose it were, suppose infant baptism to be circumcision, and circumcision infant baptism in another form: on this supposition, Saul was both baptized in infancy, and baptized after believing. He tells us that he was circumcised on the eighth day, that is, according to Pædo-baptist theory he received that which was tantamount to baptism, and yet the history before us declares that he was baptized after believing. The conclusion is, that circumcision-baptism does not supersede believer-baptism.

On this topic there is one thing more, and that of practical consequence, to which our attention is directed by the words of the narrative. They occur in Acts xxii. 16: "And now, *why tarriest thou?* arise, and be baptized". What in Saul's conduct gives occasion to this question we can only conjecture; but the doctrine which it taught him, and through him teaches ourselves, we know for certain. After a man believes, he ought to be baptized without unnecessary delay. He must not tarry. The doctrine, I said, is of practical consequence. If report speaks true, there are not a few who acknowledge, and, at the same time, neglect, the duty of being immersed. There may be cases, like that of the thief on the cross, in which the enjoyment of the ordinance is impracticable. But of all the causes of this evil, alleged or suspected, by much the most prevalent appears to be that very common and very criminal error—that the institutions of Christ may be dispensed with. I readily allow that the candidate for baptism ought to understand, as distinctly as possible, both the nature, the evidence, and the bearings of the ordinance. Precipitation has been attended with very serious consequences. By attending to baptism, whilst other doctrines, duties, or ordinances have been neglected, professors of religion have dishonoured their profession. Precipitation is one extreme; but procrastination is another. "Whosoever shall deny me before men, him will I also deny before my Father which is in heaven; and whosoever shall confess me before men, him will I confess also before my Father which is in heaven". Why tarriest thou? Death may prevent your professing your faith.

6. A few words respecting the mode of baptism, and I take leave of this instructive example.

The testimony is short, but not doubtful. Baptism must be administered, not by sprinkling, but by immersion. What is baptism? It is not sprinkling, it is washing. "Arise, and be baptized, and *wash* away thy sins". How is the person of Saul to be washed? *Answer*. By immersion. "Arise, be immersed, and, by immersion, wash away thy sins". Thus we have seen that the baptism of Paul is in perfect harmony with the commission and with the practice of the apostles.

BAPTISM OF THE CENTURION.

"And on the morrow Peter went away with them (the three messengers of Cornelius), and certain brethren from Joppa accompanied him. And the morrow after they entered into Cæsarea. And Cornelius waited for them, and had called together his kinsmen and near friends": Acts x. 23, 24.

"Now therefore (said Cornelius), are we all here present before God, to hear all things that are commanded thee of God. Then Peter opened his mouth, and said, Of a truth I perceive that God is no respecter of persons; but in every nation he that feareth him, and worketh righteousness, is accepted with him. The word which God sent unto the children of Israel, preaching peace by Jesus Christ: (he is Lord of all:) That word, I say, ye know, which was published throughout all Judæa, and began from Galilee, after the baptism which John preached; how God anointed Jesus of Nazareth with the Holy Ghost and with power; who went about doing good, and healing all that were oppressed of the devil; for God was with him. And we are witnesses of all things which he did both in the land of the Jews, and in Jerusalem; whom they slew and hanged on a tree: Him God raised up the third day, and shewed him openly, not to all the people, but unto witnesses chosen before of God, even to us, who did eat and drink with him after he rose from the dead. And he commanded us to preach unto the people, and to testify that it is he which was ordained of God to be the judge of quick and dead. To him give all the prophets witness, that through his name whosoever believeth in him shall receive remission of sins. While Peter yet spake these words, the Holy Ghost fell on all them which heard the word. And they of the circumcision which believed were astonished, as many as came with Peter, because that on the Gentiles also was poured out the gift of the Holy Ghost. For they heard them speak with tongues, and magnify God. Then answered Peter, Can any man forbid water, that these should not be baptized, which have received the Holy Ghost as well as we? And he commanded them to be baptized in the name of the Lord. Then prayed they him to tarry certain days": Acts x. 33—48.

"Who (Peter) shall tell thee words, whereby thou and all thy house shall be saved. And as I began to speak, the Holy Ghost fell on them as on us at the beginning. Then remembered I the word of the Lord, how that he said, John indeed baptized with water; but ye shall be baptized with the Holy Ghost. Forasmuch, then, as God gave them the like gift as he did unto us, who believed on the Lord Jesus Christ; what was I that I could withstand God? When they heard these things, they held their peace, and glorified God, saying, Then hath God also to the Gentiles granted repentance unto life": Acts xi. 14—18.

1. In this example we have additional evidence of *the perpetuity of water-baptism.* Some perhaps need to be informed that the perpetuity of this ordinance has been denied. The gift of the Holy Ghost, it is alleged, supersedes the necessity of water-baptism. But the opinion is erroneous. The facts in this history prove, beyond a doubt,

that *water-baptism is not superseded by the gift of the Holy Ghost.* In this case the gift of the Spirit preceded the administration of water-baptism. According to the opinion under refutation, the centurion and his relatives should not have been baptized with water, for already they had received the Spirit. But the gift of the Spirit is the very reason assigned by Peter for immersing them in water. Instead of saying that water was unnecessary, because the Gentiles had been baptized with the Holy Ghost, he says the very reverse. The words speak for themselves. "Can any man forbid water, that these should not be baptized, which have received the Holy Ghost as well as we?" "And as I began to speak, the Holy Ghost fell on them, as on us at the beginning". "Forasmuch, then, as God gave them the like gift as he did unto us, who believed on the Lord Jesus Christ; what was I, that I could withstand God?" Acts x. 47; xi. 15, 17. The inconsistency of this error with the doctrine of the example is sufficiently manifest.

2. *The design* of baptism is illustrated, as well as confirmed, by this example. It was when the Holy Ghost fell on his hearers, that Peter commanded them to be baptized. They had received the truth. The descent of the Holy Ghost was the proof, and baptism was the symbol of that reception.

3. *The qualifications* of the baptized are, according to the example, knowledge and faith. In obedience to his commission, Peter teaches or preaches before he administers baptism. Cornelius and his relatives were instructed before they were baptized. Further, previous to their baptism they

believed what they were taught. Their faith is implied in the angel's words to the centurion: "Peter shall tell thee words whereby thou and all thy house shall be saved"; and still more emphatically in the Holy Ghost falling on them. Salvation by the Gospel implies faith: "By grace are ye saved, through faith".

4. *The privileges and duties* connected with baptism are summarily comprehended in the formula, "being baptized in the name of the Lord".

5. By this example, *infants are excluded* from the ordinance of baptism. This assertion has been denied, and the baptism of Cornelius has been adduced as a plea for infant sprinkling. It is not alleged that we have express notice either of infants or of their sprinkling. It is the words of the angel that are insisted on: "Send men to Joppa, and call for Simon, whose surname is Peter; who shall tell thee words, whereby thou and all thy house shall be saved": Acts xi. 13, 14. The house of Cornelius is supposed to contain infants, and that these infants were baptized along with himself. The diligent inquirer is prepared without assistance to give the answer. The plea rests on two suppositions, both equally groundless. The first is, that there are infants in every house; the second, that infants were baptized. The supposition that there must have been infants in the house of the centurion is groundless. Everywhere there are some families without infants. The second supposition is not better supported than the first. There is no evidence that the infants (supposing that there were infants in the family), were baptized. No conclusion can be drawn from groundless

suppositions. No conscientious worshipper will observe as an institution of God that of which he cannot be fully satisfied in his own mind. Here the matter might safely be left; but there are two sentences in the history, which, separately, and much more together, determine the question from the opposite side. The "house" referred to by the angel consisted of adults. The first sentence occurs in Acts x. 24: "And Cornelius waited for them, and had called together his kinsmen and near friends". And when Peter arrived, the centurion addressed him as follows: "Now, therefore, are we all here present before God, to hear all things that are commanded thee of God". This, then, is the house of Cornelius—his kinsmen and near friends; *all present* before God, *to hear all things* that were commanded the apostle by God. The other sentence is still more decisive. It occurs in Acts xi. 14: "Peter shall tell thee words, whereby thou and all thy house shall be saved". How was the centurion to be saved? In the use of what means? By the words (the angel answers), which he should hear from Peter. And how was his house to be saved? By hearing the same words. Infants cannot be saved by hearing words. Yet all the centurion's house were saved in this way. The case is rendered, if possible, still more evident by the history of the actual administration of the ordinance. Acts x. 44: "While Peter yet spake these words, the Holy Ghost fell on all them which heard the word"—all the centurion's "kinsmen and near friends". And who, in fact, were baptized? Peter gives the answer: "Can any man forbid water, that *these* should not be baptized, which have received the Holy Ghost as well as we?" These, and none else, were baptized. They spoke with tongues, and magnified God, and prayed Peter to tarry certain days.

We learn, from this example, that infants may not be baptized, because infants cannot answer the design, possess the qualifications, discharge the duties, or enjoy the privileges connected with baptism. The baptism at Cæsarea is an example of believer-baptism; and all who acknowledge the obligation of Scripture example must acknowledge the obligation of believers to be baptized on their faith. It is objected, that if men believe, they shall be saved whether they be or be not baptized? This example makes answer, that the possession of grace is a reason for observing, not for neglecting baptism. Though Cornelius and his relatives had received the Holy Ghost, yet are they commanded to be baptized; nay, for this very reason, because they had received the Holy Ghost. This example, with those which precede, is in harmony as to the *mode* of baptism. The ground of this assertion is the primary, and in the Scriptures, the exclusive meaning of the word "*baptize*". The historian says they were baptized, that is, they were immersed in the name of the Lord.

I am called here, as in some other examples, to take notice of a very common objection. We are said to be baptized with the Holy Ghost; and in this place the Spirit is said to fall, to be poured out, to be received, to be given, in the same way in which he is said to be poured out on the day of Pentecost. Now, say the advocates for sprinkling, "is there not some resemblance supposed (when we are said to be baptized with the Holy Ghost) between these expressions and the mode of baptism?" I answer, 1. When it is said by the Baptist and by our Lord that he (Christ) should baptize with the Holy Ghost, the contrast is between the sign and the thing signified. John gave the sign; Christ gave the thing signified. 2. The expressions falling, sending, coming, resting, pouring of the Spirit, and the like, are all figurative, and cannot be used to explain the material act of baptism. Indeed, there is no resemblance between speaking different languages, healing the sick, knowing mysteries, faith, hope, charity, and the other gifts and graces of the Spirit, and either sprinkling, pouring, or immersion. The Holy Ghost, the Author of these gifts and graces, is God, and can neither be poured nor sprinkled. 3. The figures, pouring, falling, and the like, are obviously borrowed from the fine oil, water, and the other types of the Old Dispensation. They must be explained accordingly. 4. The preposition *with* literally signifies *in*. Thus, John baptized in Jordan in water, but ye shall be baptized in the Holy Ghost. Immersion is meant. 5. The mode of baptism cannot be learned from figures, but from the language and facts in the simple narratives, all of which lead us to immersion.

This example calls our attention to a topic not yet touched, namely, the *administrators* of baptism. Till now no administrator has been expressly mentioned excepting John, the disciples of Christ, the apostles, and Ananias. The words in Acts x. 48, are, "And he commanded them to be baptized in the name of the Lord". Invert the order of the words, and they intimate that the apostle, by commandment of the Lord to himself, ordered the Cæsareans to be baptized. But the inversion is both unnatural and unnecessary. The most natural meaning is, that the apostle gave orders that they should be baptized in the name of the Lord, and that he did not intend in person to baptize them, or at least all of them. On examining the context, we find that there were at Cæsarea other disciples besides Peter. "On the morrow Peter went away with them, and certain brethren from Joppa accompanied him": Acts x. 23. "Moreover, these six brethren accompanied me, and we (namely, Peter and these brethren) entered into the man's house": Acts xi. 12. It is probable, therefore, that these brethren from Joppa were the administrators. This is a hint from the Spirit which ought not to be overlooked. Amongst other practical purposes, it serves to throw light on some passages comparatively obscure. These administrators are designated neither as apostles nor elders, but simply as brethren, and if by orders of the apostles, brethren baptized at Cæsarea, they might, by the same authority, baptize at Pentecost; and they may baptize still.

Further, if men not in office may baptize, it deserves to be considered whether we are at liberty to find fault with brethren who in some extraordinary cases dispense the Supper though not invested with official authority. Something of the same kind seems to be hinted by Paul in 1 Cor. i. 13—17. "Were ye baptized in the name of Paul? I thank God that I baptized none of you, but Crispus and Gaius; lest any should say that I had baptized in mine own name. And I baptized also the household of Stephanas: besides, I know not whether I baptized any other. For Christ sent me not to baptize, but to preach the Gospel". The meaning seems to be, that Paul was chiefly employed in preaching; that the baptisms were administered most generally by his attendants, Timothy, Titus, Silas, Mark, and others, whether in office or not. Ananias, who administered baptism to Paul himself, was, for anything we know, a disciple not in office. The historian describes him merely as a disciple. It ought to be observed, that all these descriptions are given by the Spirit for practical purposes. The designation is this: "And there was a certain disciple at Damascus, named Ananias; and the Lord said unto him, Arise," &c. "And one Ananias, a devout man according to the law, having a good report of all the Jews which dwelt there, came unto me, and stood, and said unto me, Brother Saul, receive thy sight": Acts ix. 10, 11; xxii. 12, 13. The evidence is not exhausted, but enough has been said for my present purpose. Baptism is usually administered by official men; but it may also be administered by others.

LECTURE XVII.

BAPTISM OF LYDIA AND OF THE JAILOR.

"And on the Sabbath we went out of the city by a river side, where prayer was wont to be made; and we sat down, and spake unto the women which resorted thither. And a certain woman named Lydia, a seller of purple, of the city of Thyatira, which worshipped God, heard us: whose heart the Lord opened, that she attended unto the things which were spoken of Paul. And when she was baptized, and her household, she besought us, saying, If ye have judged me to be faithful to the Lord, come into my house, and abide there. And she constrained us.—And they went out of the prison, and entered into the house of Lydia: and when they had seen the brethren, they comforted them, and departed": Acts xvi. 13—15, 40.

In this example, nothing peculiar occurs on the privileges, design, perpetuity, or mode of baptism.

On these topics, I remark only, that the history of Lydia's baptism contains nothing contrary to the doctrine of the commission, or of the preceding examples; and that the truths omitted here must be supplied from these and other Scriptures. On the qualifications, duties, and subjects of the ordinance, this example is very explicit; and on the previous profession no less instructive than the case of the Ethiopian. Lydia was instructed, believed, and professed her faith, previous to baptism. In obedience to his commission, Paul begins with teaching. Lydia received his doctrine; the Lord opened her heart, that she attended unto the things which were spoken by Paul.

There is indirect, but very satisfactory, evidence, that a credible profession of faith preceded her baptism. I refer to the argument by which Lydia enforces her request that the apostle and his companions should become her guests. "And when she was baptized, and her household, she besought us, saying, If ye have judged me to be faithful to the Lord, come into my house, and abide there." When a profession of faith was made, the apostles judged of its credibility. They had heard Lydia's profession, and judged her to be faithful, and by that judgment she enforces her request: "If, (or since), ye have judged me to be faithful". The rule of receiving a Christian profession ought to be observed. Not only must a profession of faith be made and heard previous to baptism, but its credibility must be judged of and approved. Words must be employed; but if they be not credible they are not to be regarded.

The case of this woman is equally explicit as to *the subjects* of baptism. After Lydia was judged faithful, she was baptized; and every one who believes should, after her example, be baptized on his profession of faith. It ought likewise to be observed, that there was no unnecessary interval between her profession of faith and her baptism.

There is not the least evidence that infants were baptized on this occasion. In the narrative there is no mention of infants, but only of the baptism of Lydia and her household; and until it be proved that there were infants in this household, and that these infants were baptized, the cause of infant baptism is in no way supported by the narrative. A moment's attention to the facts will convince us that there is no evidence that Lydia had infants; and none, of course, that her infants were baptized. If she had infants, she would, if possible, on a journey of traffic, leave them at home; her children, if she had any, might be adult; if married, she might be childless; her household might consist of adult friends, or of her servants who assisted her in the manufacture of purple. Her whole language inclines one to believe, especially if acquainted with the manners of the East, that she was not married.

I said, therefore, that in this example there is no mention of infants, or of their baptism. Unproved suppositions must never be mistaken for facts.

BAPTISM OF THE JAILOR.

"And when they had laid many stripes upon them (Paul and Silas), they cast them into prison, charging the jailor to keep them safely: who having received such a charge, thrust them into the inner prison, and made their feet fast in the stocks. And at midnight Paul and Silas prayed, and sang praises unto God: and the prisoners heard them. And suddenly there was a great earthquake, so that the foundations of the prison were shaken: and immediately all the doors were opened, and every one's bands were loosed. And the keeper of the prison awaking out of his sleep, and seeing the prison doors open, he drew out his sword, and would have killed himself, supposing that the prisoners had been fled. But Paul cried with a loud voice, saying, Do thyself no harm: for we are all here. Then he called for a light, and sprang in, and came trembling, and fell down before Paul and Silas, and brought them out, and said, Sirs, what must I do to be saved? And they said, Believe on the Lord Jesus Christ, and thou shalt be saved, and thy house. And they spake unto him the word of the Lord, and to all that were in his house. And he took them the same hour of the night, and washed their stripes; and was baptized, he and all his, straightway. And when he had brought them into his house, he set meat before them, and rejoiced, believing in God with all his house. And when it was day, the magistrates sent the serjeants, saying, Let those men go. And the keeper of the prison told this saying to Paul, The magistrates have sent to let you go: now, therefore, depart, and go in peace." Acts xvi. 23—36.

Nothing peculiar occurs in this history on the perpetuity, design, privileges, duties, or mode of baptism: but it confirms the doctrine of the preceding examples respecting the qualifications and subjects of the ordinance; and teaches us what ideas we ought to attach to the expression, "baptized households".

What are the qualifications for baptism? If we are to take the answer from this approved pattern, these qualifications are knowledge and faith. Verses 30—34: "And he (the jailor) said, What must I do to be saved? And they said, Believe on the Lord Jesus Christ, and thou shalt be saved, and thy house. And they spake unto him the word of the Lord, and to all that were in his house. And he . . then was baptized, he and all his, straightway, . . on and rejoiced, believing in God with all his house". He was convicted, he was instructed, he believed, and was baptized.

Is it the duty of every believer to be baptized? The narrative answers in the affirmative, and confirms the doctrine of the immediate connection between baptism and faith. No interval of time, without necessity, must occur between believing and being baptized. The language here is very expressive of this doctrine. Straightway, the same hour of the night, without any interval, he was baptized. The friends of religion who are tempted to procrastination will do well to consider this language.

To the expression, " baptized household ", what ideas are we to attach? The narrative answers explicitly: Not the idea of infancy, but of grace, and of grace exercised and professed: verses 30—34.

Further, the apostles say, in verse 31, " Believe on the Lord Jesus Christ, and thou shalt be saved, *and thy house*". Do they mean the jailor's wife, and infants, and adult children, and servants, and their infants, should all be saved, whether they themselves had faith or had it not, provided only that *he*, the head of the family, believed? Are we thus to understand the apostles? Or are we to understand them as saying that, if he believed, he should be saved, and that if any, or all of his household should believe, they should be saved in the same way with himself? In the first sense, say the abettors of infant sprinkling; the Anti-pædo-baptists say in the latter. The historian gives the answer, and by his answer teaches us how we are to understand similar words wherever they occur in the sacred history. The words of the historian, in verse 32, are, " And they spake unto him the word of the Lord, and to all that were in his house ". The word of the Lord was spoken *to all* that were in his house; of course they could hear and understand it; then they were not infants. The historian proceeds, in verse 34 : " And he rejoiced, believing in God with all his house". All his house rejoiced in God, all his house believed in God; they were neither graceless, nor unbelievers, nor infants; but sanctified persons, believing and professing their faith. Thus the Holy Spirit has taught us how he wishes to be understood, when he speaks of "baptized households"—of men believing, and being saved with their houses; and, in particular, how we are to understand the account of the baptism of the household of Lydia.

The remarks formerly made on the subject of households confirm this conclusion. Households were baptized when they believed, and not otherwise.

The cause of infant baptism is not supported by the case of the jailor. The words of the narrative speak nothing of infants. They record the conversion and consequent baptism of the jailor and his house. The whole is an example and a proof, that, after faith, the believer ought to be baptized; but in no way does it give any sanction to the baptism of infants.

A text of like import is quoted from 1 Cor. i. 16: "And I baptized also the household of Stephanas". These words speak nothing of infants, and consequently can furnish no proof of their baptism. Allow me to read 1 Cor. xvi. 15, 16: "I beseech you, brethren, (ye know the house of Stephanas, that it is the firstfruits of Achaia, and that they have addicted themselves to the ministry of the saints), that ye submit yourselves unto such". The household of Stephanas, you see, were not only believers, but believers of distinction, ministering to the saints, and entitled to their submission. I need not repeat the consequence; this evidence, like the rest, subverts the cause which it is adduced to support. Under the head of households some other passages have been mentioned; but the inquirer, on reading them, will, without assistance, perceive, that, if possible, they are even less to the point for infant baptism than the histories of Stephanas and the jailor. But before leaving this topic, two or three remarks may be of use.

1. First, the word *household*, in connection with baptism, must signify the believing part of the household. The reasons are such as follow:—(1), The commission and consequent practice of the apostles limit baptism to a profession of faith. (2), Two of the three baptized houses are expressly adult, and oblige us to understand the house of Lydia as adult also. (3), The households saluted by the apostles are adults, for they are supposed to be capable of receiving the salutations. Take the word household in connection with baptism as restricted to believers, and all is scriptural and plain; but take the word in the Pædo-baptist sense, that is, unrestricted, and mark the consequence. The household is baptized on the faith of its head; that is, the infant part of the children, the adult part of the children, the relative inmates, the slaves, the servants; the whole household, like the infants, are baptized or sprinkled on the faith of the parent or master. Shall we admit all these, or reject part of them? If the Pædo-baptist answer, Admit; his practice refutes his answer. If he say, Reject; his plea is gone; its force lies in the unlimited sense of the word. In a word, if the

household is to be baptized on the faith of its head, how are we to dispose of the part of it that is unbelieving, but willing to be baptized or sprinkled on the call of its superior?

2. Further, The sacred historians have nowhere said that the apostles baptized believers with their households. They say, indeed, that the houses of Lydia, Stephanas, and the jailor, were baptized; but this is a thing very different from a general assertion, both in itself and its consequences. The general assertion would have indicated that to baptize believers and their households was the usual practice of the apostles. But the general assertion does not occur; it is studiously avoided, and the reason must be that this was not their practice. The house of the jailor is mentioned, and perhaps the other two, because they were extraordinary cases; had they been ordinary, or had the general assertion been used, it is not probable that particulars would have been recorded; and it is still less likely that they would have been recorded without some intimation that they were instances of a general practice. Take an example of the historian's language in a similar case. The apostle went into the synagogue, "*as his manner was*".

This remark detects the fallacy of one of the most plausible pleas for pædo-baptism. It is alleged, that multitudes of households were baptized by the Apostles, and that it is altogether improbable that there were infants in none of them. But the reverse of this is the doctrine of the sacred historians. They avoid the general assertion that the apostles baptized households; they mention three extraordinary cases; two of the three are declared to be adult. Instead of a multitude of households, we have the house of Lydia only, and to it I must apply a common rule of interpretation: "The more obscure must be explained by the more clear Scriptures". Judging by the houses of Stephanas and the jailor, I conclude that the house of Lydia believed. The conclusion is strengthened by a degree of positive evidence. Acts xvi. 40: "And they (the apostles) went out of the prison, and entered into the house of Lydia: and when they had seen the brethren, they comforted them, and departed." Whether these brethren consisted of Lydia and her household only, or of others along with them, they are all described as comforted, that is, as receiving comfort as believers.

3. Our last remark here is that a believing household may be restricted to two or three of its members. A whole, in the language of Scripture, is often used for a part; thus, all Judea is said to be baptized of John, and yet Christ is said to make more disciples than John. The whole is used for a part of Judea.

On this principle, the believer's household is that part of it, whether great or small, partaking of like precious faith with the head. It must be restricted to believers, and it need not be extended beyond the lowest plurality.

The sum of these remarks is, that the apostles did not usually baptize households; that the households baptized were few; that, without perhaps a single exception, the baptized households are described as believers. In a word, the sacred record of baptized households furnishes no proof of pædo-baptism.

LECTURE XVIII.

BAPTISMS AT CORINTH, UNTO MOSES, AT EPHESUS, AND AT ROME.

"And he departed thence, and entered into a certain man's house, named Justus, one that worshipped God, whose house joined hard to the synagogue. And Crispus, the chief ruler of the synagogue, believed on the Lord with all his house; and many of the Corinthians hearing, believed, and were baptized": Acts xviii. 7, 8.

"For it hath been declared unto me of you, my brethren; by them which are of the house of Chloe, that there are contentions among you. Now this I say, that every one of you saith, I am of Paul; and I of Apollos; and I of Cephas, and I of Christ. Is Christ divided? was Paul crucified for you? or were ye baptized in the name of Paul? I thank God that I baptized none of you, but Crispus and Gaius; lest any should say that I had baptized in mine own name. And I baptized also the household of Stephanas: besides, I know not whether I baptized any other. For Christ sent me not to baptize, but to preach the Gospel": 1 Cor. i. 11—17.

"Moreover, brethren, I would not that ye should be ignorant, how that all our fathers were under the cloud, and all passed through the sea; and were all baptized unto Moses in the cloud and in the sea": 1 Cor. x. 1, 2.

"Else what shall they do which are baptized for the dead, if the dead rise not at all? why are they then baptized for the dead?" 1 Cor. xv. 29.

BAPTISMS AT CORINTH. 209

"I beseech you, brethren, (ye know the house of Stephanas, that it is the first fruits of Achaia, and that they have addicted themselves to the ministry of the saints,) that ye submit yourselves unto such": 1 Cor. xvi. 15, 16.

1. The record here harmonises with the commission and the preceding examples. It both illustrates and confirms the doctrine of *the design* of baptism. The historian tells us "that Crispus, the chief ruler of the synagogue, believed on the Lord, with all his house; and that many of the Corinthians hearing, believed, and were baptized". The baptism of the Corinthians signified that they believed what they had heard; and although the baptism of the household of Crispus be not mentioned, yet there is no doubt that they also were special examples of the design of baptism, as a symbol of the application of the truth to the individuals baptized. The same doctrine is illustrated and confirmed in the account of the divisions or schisms at Corinth. "Is Christ divided? was Paul crucified for you? or were ye baptized *in the name of Paul?* I thank God that I baptized none of you, but Crispus and Gaius: lest any should say, that I had baptized *in mine own name.*" The words, "in the name," are the same here as in the commission. Their import is plainly this, that had the Corinthians been baptized into the name of Apollos or Cephas, their being so baptized would have signified that they were to take their instructions from Apollos or Cephas. Had the Corinthians been baptized into the name of Paul, their being so baptized would have signified that they acknowledged Paul for their ruler, and that they

purposed to take their instructions from him. On the same principle, their being baptized into the name of Christ signified that they acknowledged Christ as their teacher, and purposed to take all their instructions from him.

We have another striking illustration of the design of baptism in the account of the Israelites passing through the Red Sea: "Moreover, brethren, I would not that ye should be ignorant, how that all our fathers were under the cloud, and all passed through the sea; and were all baptized unto Moses in the cloud and in the sea". The preposition is the same as in the passage last quoted and in the commission. This baptism *in, into*, or *unto* Moses, plainly implies that they followed Moses under the cloud and through the Red Sea, in the faith that he was a leader sent them from God, and that they intended to be guided by his authority. The words in the Old Testament history are these: "Thus the Lord saved Israel that day out of the hand of the Egyptians; and Israel saw the Egyptians dead upon the sea-shore. And Israel saw that great work which the Lord did upon the Egyptians; and the people feared the Lord, and believed the Lord, and his servant Moses": Exod. xiv. 30, 31. This they did before; but their faith was confirmed by this event. Their passing through the sea, under the cloud, was the symbol of their faith. It was their "baptism *unto* Moses": they acknowledged him to be the servant appointed by the Lord to instruct and lead them. Our baptism into Christ is of the same import. It is the symbol that we receive him as our Prophet, Priest, and King.

2. *The qualifications* of the baptized, according to the narrative of the baptisms at Corinth, are knowledge and faith. In obedience to his commission, Paul commenced his labours by preaching at Corinth. "After these things Paul departed from Athens, and came to Corinth. And he reasoned in the synagogue every Sabbath, and persuaded the Jews and Greeks, and testified to the Jews that Jesus was the Christ". His labours were blessed, and many believed. "And Crispus, the chief ruler of the synagogue, believed on the Lord, with all his house; and many of the Corinthians hearing, believed, and were baptized".

3. *The privileges* of the baptized, also, are illustrated by the example. "If Christ be not raised, your faith is vain, ye are yet in your sins. Then they also which are fallen asleep in Christ are perished": 1 Cor. xv. 17, 18. If Christ be not raised, "what shall they do which are baptized for the dead, (for Christ), if the dead rise not at all? why are they then baptized for the dead" (which Christ must be) if there be no resurrection? (verse 29.) Their baptism into Christ represents their deliverance from sin and all its consequences. Their baptism for one for ever dead would have been vain. If they were baptized for the dead, they were yet in their sins. But if Christ were risen, their baptism represented that they were no longer in their sins; their hopes of salvation were not in vain. Such are the privileges of the baptized according to this example, and these privileges are also illustrated by the Israelites' baptism unto Moses. The deliverance of the literal Israel typified and prefigured the deliverance of such as are Israelites indeed.

On *the duties* of the baptized this example contains nothing peculiar, except that the baptism of the Israelites unto Moses represented their obligations to obey him, as our baptism into Christ represents our obligations to follow and obey him.

4. This example confirms the doctrine of the necessity of being baptized without unnecessary delay, *after* we have believed. Between our faith and our baptism no unnecessary delay ought to intervene. Like the Corinthians, hearing, we should believe; and believing, we should be baptized.

The passage quoted from the 10th chapter of First Corinthians has been urged in support of infant sprinkling. The children passed through the sea along with their parents, and neither the one nor the other were plunged into it; they were sprinkled by the cloud, but not immersed in the sea. Supposing that this assertion were true, it will not follow that, under the Gospel, infants ought to be sprinkled. Corporeal acts suited a carnal dispensation, and prefigured a dispensation that requires the worship of God in spirit and in truth. The fact, however, is misrepresented. The Scriptures, neither by Moses nor by Paul, speak of the Israelites being sprinkled. Paul says they were *immersed* in the sea and in the cloud. As to the children passing through the sea with their parents, it no more proves that children ought to be baptized, than the passage of the mixed multitude and the cattle with the Israelites proves an absurdity too gross to be mentioned. As to the *mode*, Paul everywhere uses the word "baptize", which signifies to immerse. As to the *subjects*, the narrative is particular, it is even minute; but it makes no mention of infants or of their baptism. "And Crispus, the chief ruler of the synagogue, believed on the Lord with all his house; and many of the Corinthians hearing, believed, and were baptized"—why not add—*with their infants?* Every thing required the addition, had infants been baptized. It is, however, not made. There can be but one reason:—No infants were baptized at Corinth.

Before I conclude these remarks, allow me to repeat the remark, that by the words, "baptized households", we must understand the believing part of the household. The household of Crispus was, I have no doubt, baptized; but the household of Crispus believed. "And Crispus, the chief ruler of the synagogue, believed on the Lord, with all his house." The conversion of a whole household was, even under the preaching of the apostles, no ordinary occurrence. When it did occur, it is recorded; sometimes, as here, under the head of faith; and sometimes under the head of baptism. The Spirit has thus taught us, by circumstantial description, how we are to understand his more summary and general expressions.

BAPTISMS AT EPHESUS.

"And it came to pass, that, while Apollos was at Corinth, Paul having passed through the upper coasts came to Ephesus; and finding certain disciples, he said unto them, Have ye received the Holy Ghost since ye believed? And they said unto him, We have not so much as heard whether there be any Holy Ghost. And he said unto them, Unto what then were ye baptized? And they said, Unto John's baptism. Then said Paul, John verily baptized with the baptism of repentance, saying unto the people, that they should believe on him which should come after him, that is, on Christ Jesus. When they heard this, they were baptized in the name of the Lord Jesus. And when Paul had laid his hands upon them, the Holy Ghost came on them; and they spake with tongues, and prophesied. And all the men were about twelve": Acts xix. 1—7.

"There is one body, and one Spirit, even as ye are called in one hope of your calling; one Lord, one faith, one baptism": Eph. iv. 4.

1. *The design* of baptism, both as to matter and expression, is here exhibited nearly as in the commission. They were baptized in the name of the Lord Jesus. These Ephesians were baptized into the faith, hope, and obedience of the Gospel. Their baptism was a symbol of the application of the truth to themselves. As John taught that men should believe in Christ when he should come, so the Apostles taught that men should believe in him as having actually come.

2. *The qualifications* for baptism, according to this example, are the knowledge and belief of this truth. "Then said Paul, John verily baptized with the baptism of repentance, saying unto the people, that they should believe on him which should come after him, that is, on Christ Jesus. When they heard this they were baptized in the name of the Lord Jesus." They heard and believed what Paul told them; and in evidence that they believed, they were baptized. Respecting the privileges of the baptized, it is stated that the Ephesians received the Holy Ghost.

3. This narrative increases the evidence that men after believing ought to be baptized without unnecessary delay. As soon as these disciples heard Paul's discourse, they believed, and were baptized. "When they heard this they were baptized in the name of the Lord Jesus." The mode of administering the ordinance is the same as before: these disciples were baptized, that is, according to the meaning of the word, they were immersed into the name of the Lord Jesus.

There are two peculiarities in this case, and before we leave it, their bearings on practice must be noticed. (1.) These twelve men were twice baptized, once into John's baptism and afterwards into the name of the Lord Jesus. The difference between these baptisms has been noticed; and though it was comparatively small, the one baptism did not supersede the necessity of the other. Let it be recollected that infant sprinkling is no baptism, and we have satisfactory evidence that, although sprinkled in infancy, we are bound, like these Ephesians, to be baptized in the name of the Lord Jesus.

(2.) The unity of baptism forms the other peculiarity. The apostle says, "There is one Lord, one faith, one baptism." According to this doctrine, either the baptism of believers, or of infants, must be rejected. The immersion of believers is scriptural baptism, and as there is but *one* baptism, that of infants must be rejected.

We have an account of twelve men baptized at Ephesus, but none of infant sprinkling.

BAPTISM OF THE ROMANS.

"What shall we say then? Shall we continue in sin, that grace may abound? God forbid. How shall we that are dead to sin, live any longer therein? Know ye not, that so many of us as were baptized into Jesus Christ, were baptized into his death? Therefore we are buried with him by baptism into death. that like as Christ was raised up from the dead by the glory of the Father, even so we also should walk in newness of life. . . Likewise reckon ye also yourselves to be dead indeed unto sin, but alive unto God, through Jesus Christ our Lord": Rom. vi. 1—4, 11.

1. This passage harmonizes with the commission as to *the design* of baptism. It is the symbol of the application of the truth to the individual baptized. To be baptized into the death of Christ is by our baptism to signify that we receive for practical purposes the truth concerning his death. On this design of their baptism, accordingly, Paul founds his exhortations to the baptized Romans. Had not the application of the truth to the baptized been represented by their baptism, the exhortations would be misapplied.

2. *The qualifications* for baptism, according to this passage, are understanding and faith. To be baptized into the death of Christ implies, that the truth respecting Christ in general, and his death and resurrection in particular, is understood and believed.

3. Both *the privileges and duties* connected with baptism are here strongly marked. The privilege is implied in the words read, and expressed in the

14th verse: "For sin shall not have dominion over you: for ye are not under the law, but under grace."

4. *The duties* are repeatedly expressed in the context. Verse 4: "Therefore we are buried with him by baptism into death: that like as Christ was raised up from the dead by the glory of the Father, even so we also should walk in newness of life." Verses 12 and 13: "Let not sin therefore reign in your mortal body, that ye should obey it in the lusts thereof; neither yield ye your members as instruments of unrighteousness unto sin: but yield yourselves unto God, as those that are alive from the dead, and your members as instruments of righteousness unto God." On both the privileges and duties connected with baptism the context is full and explicit.

Infant sprinkling receives no countenance from this passage. The apostle is guarding the Romans against abusing the doctrine of justification by free grace: "What shall we say then? Shall we continue in sin, that grace may abound?" He urges their baptism as a motive to the contrary: "Let not sin, therefore, reign in your mortal body." Infants are incapable of using or abusing the doctrines of grace, and equally incapable of being influenced by motives taken from baptism. The apostle's words contain a clause which goes directly to exclude infants.—" Know ye not, that *so many of us* as were baptized into Jesus Christ, were baptized into his death?" Not a person, therefore, had been baptized at Rome who was not capable of listening to the exhortations in this chapter. But this is not all. Paul classes himself with these

Romans; he classes himself with all the baptized throughout the world: "Know ye not that as many of us," (us baptized Christians). There was not a baptized individual throughout the world who was not concerned in these things; no infant, of course, had, when this epistle was written, been admitted to baptism. In chapter 15th, verse 19, the apostle tells us how many had become disciples: "So that from Jerusalem, and round about unto Illyricum, I have fully preached the Gospel of Christ." Yet throughout all this extent of the world, and during the thirty years that had elapsed since Christ entered on his public ministry, not a single infant had been baptized: "Know ye not, that so many of us as have been baptized into Jesus Christ, have been baptized into his death."

The language of this passage is so descriptive of immersion that it has attracted general attention. To baptize is to immerse. "Know ye not, that so many of us as were immersed into Jesus Christ were immersed into his death; therefore we are buried with him by immersion into death, that like as Christ was raised up from the dead by the glory of the Father, even so we also should walk in newness of life; for if we have been planted together in the likeness of his death, we shall be also in the likeness of his resurrection." There are two objections, but neither of them of consequence. As to that drawn from the matter, it may be asked, why this language was used? the matter could have been expressed in different language. As to that drawn from the 5th verse,—"That a similar use of figures frequently occurs in the Scriptures"; the figure in the 5th verse is obviously employed to strengthen the idea in the 4th verse,—our union with Christ, and conformity to him in his death, burial, and resurrection, represented by immersion in water, and rising out of it. It has been well said, that had not baptism been administered by immersion, we had never heard of these expressions, being *buried* with him by immersion into death, and *rising* with him to newness of life. The language is in harmony with all that has hitherto occurred on the mode of baptism. The symbol graphically describes the truths which it is employed to represent. The words and the facts of Scripture prove that baptism was, in the time of the apostles, administered by immersion, and such allusions as these in the passage before us tend not a little to strengthen the proof.

I have only to add, that if our conduct is to be determined by the examples in Scripture, we must be baptized after believing. The converts at Rome believed, and were baptized in testimony of their faith and its consequences.

LECTURE XIX.

BAPTISMS IN GALATIA, AT COLOSSE, AND I PET. III. 18—21.

"But after that faith is come, we are no longer under a schoolmaster. For ye are all the children of God by faith in Christ Jesus. For as many of you as have been baptized into Christ have put on Christ. There is neither Jew nor Greek, there is neither bond nor free, there is neither male nor female: for ye are all one in Christ Jesus. And if ye be Christ's, then are ye Abraham's seed, and heirs according to the promise": Gal. iii. 25—29.

1. *The design* of baptism, to represent the application of the truth to the baptized, is graphically described in these words, "putting on Christ." The righteousness of Christ is a robe. This robe is held out to all who hear the Gospel, and is received and put on by believers. "But now the righteousness of God without the law is manifested, being witnessed by the law and the prophets. Even the righteousness of God which is by faith of Christ Jesus, unto all and *upon* all them that believe": Rom. iii. 21. "I counsel thee to buy of me white raiment, that thou mayest be clothed, and that the shame of thy nakedness do not appear": Rev. iii. 18. The Lord's people are all comely through his comeliness put upon them; being clothed, they are not found naked. They

put on Christ, and baptism is the symbol of this clothing : " For as many of you as have been baptized into Christ, have put on Christ." There is no difference of nation, of sex, of Gentile, or Jew; so plainly is the mystical union and its consequences exhibited in baptism. How do men put on the righteousness of Christ ? By what is the union formed ? The answer is, By faith : " By grace are ye saved, through faith." This faith is represented in baptism, and is accordingly *the qualification* for the ordinance. This qualification is both implied and expressed : " But after that *faith* is come, we are no longer under a schoolmaster. For ye are all the children of God by faith in Christ Jesus. For as many of you as have been baptized into Christ, have put on Christ." By *faith* the Galatians were qualified for baptism.

2. *The privileges* of the baptized are clearly exhibited. For instance, adoption : "For ye are all the children of God by faith in Christ Jesus. And if ye be Christ's, then are ye Abraham's seed, and heirs according to the promise." All the benefits of the covenant of grace are inseparably connected; whoever, therefore, is adopted, enjoys all the benefits of the covenant. On this head, the passage accords with the commission and with all the preceding examples. The same must be said of *the duties*. "*Christ*" signifies the things concerning Christ; not some, but all of them; not the things respecting imputed righteousness merely, but the things of duty also; all things whatsoever Christ has commanded us. To put on Christ, therefore, is, in consequence of union to him, to imitate his holy example. Rom. xiii. 12—14 : "The night is

far spent, the day is at hand: let us therefore *cast off* the works of darkness, and let us *put on* the armour of light. Let us walk honestly, as in the day; not in rioting and drunkenness, not in chambering and wantonness, not in strife and envying. But put ye on the Lord Jesus Christ, and make not provision for the flesh, to fulfil the lusts thereof". These duties are incumbent on the baptized: "For as many of you as have been baptized into Christ have put on Christ": Gal. iii. 27.

3. Infant baptism cannot be inferred from this passage, or from the context; nothing is said of infants or of their baptism. On the contrary, this passage directly excludes infants from baptism. The apostle tells us that every individual who had been baptized in the regions of Galatia, had put on Christ; none else were baptized.* It is worthy of being remarked, that the very same language is employed to describe the baptisms at Rome. The procedure of the first administrators was uniform; what they did in the city of Rome, the metropolis of the world, and what they did in the extensive regions of Galatia, they did everywhere. They baptized none who had not put on Christ. The consequence is plain; none ought to be baptized who have not put on Christ. Infants cannot, therefore, be baptized. It is not a little presumptuous to oppose to these striking conclusions

---

* The apostle takes for granted the sincerity of their profession; false brethren might have unawares crept in, but it was meet for him to think this of all the baptized, that they were partakers of the grace which he had received. See Phil. i. 7.—J. H.

imaginary inferences from abrogated institutions.

4. On the mode of baptism there is nothing peculiar; but what we have favours immersion. Expressions similar to those under consideration frequently occur. Thus we read of "putting off the body of the sins of the flesh"; "of putting off the old man, and putting on the new man"; of "putting on the Lord Jesus Christ". These figures appear to be very bold; but when we view them as borrowed from immersion their meaning becomes very plain. Baptism is the symbol of the practical reception of the truth by the baptized. The rejection of evil, and the purpose and practice of good, are therefore naturally expressed by putting off the one and putting on the other. A very early and general custom connected with this ordinance illustrates the language employed. The baptized, after immersion, were clothed with a change of raiment, expressive of the great change they had undergone. But, altogether apart from this unauthorized custom, the word *baptize* signifies *to immerse*, and the language before us is fully descriptive of the mode of administering the ordinance.

Before quitting the case of the Galatians, I must not omit a very important purpose to which these remarks ought to be applied; to answer, I mean, some objections drawn from the context, verses 13, 14, 17: "Christ hath redeemed us from the curse of the law, being made a curse for us; for it is written, Cursed is every one that hangeth on a tree. That the blessing of Abraham might come on the Gentiles through Jesus Christ; that we might receive the promise of the Spirit through faith.* And this I say, that the covenant that was confirmed before of God in Christ, the law, which was four hundred and thirty years after, cannot disannul, that it should make the promise of none effect." From these words, by a process of ratiocination not to be understood, infant baptism has been inferred.† But the fact that those, and those only, were baptized, who had put on Christ, proves that the inference must be false, and supersedes the necessity of quoting and confuting the visionary speculations of Pædo-baptists.

BAPTISMS AT COLOSSE.

"And ye are complete in him, which is the head of all principality and power; in whom also ye are circumcised with the circumcision made without hands, in putting off the body of the sins of the flesh by the circumcision of Christ:

---

* The blessing of Abraham, or of justification by faith, and every other spiritual blessing, is conveyed to believers through the death of Christ, into the faith of which they are baptized, and thus their union with him is exhibited. The believer puts on Christ in the lowest state of his humiliation; and he shall also be a partaker of the glory which shall be revealed. When Christ who is our life shall appear, we shall also appear with him in glory.—J. H.

† The doctrine of justification by faith had been unalterably settled by God's covenant with Abraham. It was also confirmed by the token of the covenant, that the great object of his faith, the Saviour of sinners, should spring from this eminent patriarch; and the law, which was 430 years after, could not disannul what had been thus irrevocably fixed. The great object of the apostle was to confirm the Galatians in the doctrine of justification by faith, in opposition to the Judaizing teachers; but it is not easy to perceive how this can be supposed to bear upon the baptism of infants.—J. H.

Buried with him in baptism, wherein also ye are risen with him through the faith of the operation of God, who hath raised him from the dead. And you, being dead in your sins, and the uncircumcision of your flesh, hath he quickened together with him, having forgiven you all trespasses. Blotting out the handwriting of ordinances that was against us, which was contrary to us, and took it out of the way, nailing it to his cross": Col. ii. 10—14.

1. *The design* of baptism is implied in these words. Whoever receives the truth is, by faith, united to Christ, who thus takes up his abode in the heart: Eph. iii. 17. The symbol of this is baptism. United to Christ by faith, believers become interested in his death, burial, and resurrection. By baptism into death, they are buried, and raised to walk with Christ in newness of life. In substance, this is the same as being baptized into the name of the Father, Son, and Holy Ghost.

2. *The qualifications* for baptism here specified are regeneration and faith.

The Colossians had the Christian circumcision, the circumcision which Christ requires, and which he effects, not by the hands of men, but by the influences of his own Spirit. The Colossians believed; they had risen with Christ through the faith of the operation of God. The Colossians, therefore, were qualified according to the commission, and, being so qualified, were baptized.

3. *The privileges* connected with baptism are the same as in the preceding examples; forgiveness, sanctification, and protection are specified. "Buried with him in baptism, wherein also ye are risen with him, through the faith of the operation

of God, who hath raised him from the dead. And you, being dead in your sins and the uncircumcision of your flesh, hath he quickened together with him, having forgiven you all trespasses. Blotting out the handwriting of ordinances that was against us, which was contrary to us, and took it out of the way, nailing it to his cross; and having spoiled principalities and powers, he made a show of them openly, triumphing over them in it."

4. *The duties* of mortification and vivification, or dying to sin and living to righteousness, are implied in being buried with Christ and rising with him. These Colossians are examples of men being baptized after believing. The passage speaks nothing of the baptism of infants. As to *the mode* of baptism, the words imply immersion. Immersion does, and sprinkling does not, represent our burial and resurrection with Christ. Being put under the water gives a striking representation of death and burial; rising out of the water gives a striking representation of resurrection, whether to newness of life, or to glory. Whoever considers these things, and compares the language in this epistle with the language in the epistle to the Romans, (ch. vi. 3.) can hardly fail to perceive that the figure in both is taken from the mode of baptism by immersion.

Before quitting this passage, it will be expected by such as are acquainted with the Baptist Controversy that I would take notice of the inference that has been drawn from it in favour of Pædobaptism. It has been supposed that by the "circumcision of Christ", baptism is meant. On this supposition it is argued, "If baptism be circumcision, and circumcision baptism, infants must be baptized now, as they were circumcised under the law." On the circumcision question I am not here to enter, except so far as this passage is concerned.

In reply, I observe (1.) That the example is not in harmony with the inference. According to the inference, infants must be baptized; according to the example, they ought not to be baptized. Every one baptized at Colosse was a believer. They were circumcised with the circumcision made without hands; they had risen with Christ through the faith of the operation of God. There is no exception made in case of infancy.

I observe (2) It is not baptism that is called the circumcision of Christ. The words are, "In whom also ye are circumcised with the circumcision made without hands, in putting off the body of the sins of the flesh, by the circumcision of Christ."* That is, you Colossians need not be circumcised, for you have already received the circumcision of Christ, when you received the circumcision made without hands, when you were regenerated, when you put off the body of the sins of the flesh. The place is parallel to Romans ii. 28, 29 : "For he is not a Jew, which is one outwardly; neither is that circumcision, which is outward in the flesh; but he is a Jew which is one inwardly; and circumcision is that of the heart, in the spirit, and not in the letter; whose praise is not of men, but of God" It is this spiritual circumcision, this regeneration, this putting off the body of the sins of the flesh; it is this,—it is not baptism,—which is the

---

* Baptism is not made without hands, and cannot, therefore, be the circumcision here spoken of.—J. H.

circumcision of Christ. Baptism is the symbol of this regeneration, and therefore it follows in the next verse,—" Buried with him in baptism, wherein also ye are risen with him through the faith of the operation of God, who hath raised him from the dead." The words, " the circumcision of Christ," belong to the 11th verse. The word " baptism " belongs to the 12th verse. The words " circumcision of Christ," are connected with what goes before, not with what follows after. We are not therefore taught here, (nor indeed anywhere else,) that baptism is circumcision, or circumcision baptism. The Colossians are taught that they did not need the Jewish circumcision, because in their regeneration they had the antitype of circumcision, the circumcision of Christ.*

I observe (3) That although we were to suppose that baptism were called circumcision, yet it would be so called only in the way of allusion, as praise is called sacrifice, and Christians called Jews, or the circumcision. Though Christians are called Jews, (Rom. ii. 29), none are so foolish as to imagine that therefore Christians are under the law of Moses ; though praise is called sacrifice, none are so foolish as to imagine that our praises are under the rules of the ancient sacrifices ; and although, in the way of allusion, baptism were called circumcision, it would be equally foolish to suppose that baptism is to be regulated by the laws of circumcision.

---

* What the apostle terms the circumcision of Christ, is that circumcision promised to Israel : Deut. xxx. 6. It is the *true*, the *inward* circumcision; in other words, the taking away the stony heart out of their flesh, and giving them an heart of flesh.—J. H.

I observe (4) That although baptism really were circumcision, and circumcision baptism, it does not follow that baptism is to be regulated by the laws of circumcision. In some things the rule is certainly altered; females, for example, are to be baptized. In how many more particulars it is altered we must learn from the New Testament. In other words, we must take all our information respecting baptism from the record of the New Dispensation, and not from the law of Moses.

PETER'S REFERENCE TO BAPTISM.

"For Christ also hath once suffered for sins, the just for the unjust, that he might bring us to God, being put to death in the flesh, but quickened by the Spirit: by which also he went and preached unto the spirits in prison; which sometime were disobedient, when once the longsuffering of God waited in the days of Noah, while the ark was a preparing, wherein few, that is, eight souls, were saved by water. The like figure whereunto even baptism doth also now save us (not the putting away of the filth of the flesh, but the answer of a good conscience toward God,) by the resurrection of Jesus Christ": 1 Pet. iii. 18—21.

1. *One qualification* for baptism is here expressly stated, namely, the answer of a good conscience towards God; this therefore is a qualification for baptism universally necessary.

2. *The privileges* connected with baptism are explicitly stated under the term *salvation*. Eight souls were saved by water; the like figure whereunto even baptism doth also now save us, by the

resurrection of Jesus Christ; that is, baptism is the symbol of salvation to every one who is baptized, with the answer of a good conscience. There is no exception. The exclusion of infants from baptism is as decisively intimated here, as their exclusion from the Supper is in 1 Cor. xi. Why are infants debarred from the Lord's Supper? Because, it is answered, they cannot discern the Lord's body, or examine themselves. And why are infants debarred from baptism? Because they cannot have the answer of a good conscience. Whatever is urged in answer to objections in the one case may be urged in answer to objections in the other.

3. *The necessity of baptism* is implied in the words under consideration. The language is very strong—"Baptism doth also now save us."* The words are parallel, in this respect, to John iii. 5. The same truth is implied in Mark xvi. 16, and Rom. x. 10. A man in certain circumstances, like the thief on the cross, may be saved without baptism; but the circumstances must be peculiar which render baptism unnecessary. Were any man willingly and obstinately to contemn the ordinance, there could be no scriptural hope of his

---

* To me it seems that Peter speaks of Baptism as another *figure* of salvation, similar to that of the ark. I should not venture to detach the sentence and place it as it stands in the above paragraph. Our author speaks very strongly in the following sentences; but his spirit and life prevent our imputing to him any doubt as to the salvation of his unbaptized brethren, who remained so because they did not see it to be their Lord's will. Neither did he attribute any saving power to water-baptism in and of itself.—C. H. S.

salvation. The consequence leads us to the uniform doctrine of the New Testament—after believing we must be baptized. The question is practical, and must, by conscientious men, be considered with a view to practice.

Baptism in ordinary cases is connected with salvation. Every believer therefore must be baptized on his faith.

4. Further, the ordinance of baptism is *permanent;* there is no limitation as to time, either here or anywhere else. It is an error, therefore, to limit the ordinance to proselytes, or men converted from amongst heathens or Jews. Since baptism is a permanent ordinance, and connected with salvation, the connection must continue to the end of the world.

5. *The mode* of baptism is immersion. "The like figure whereunto (the ark in the deluge) even baptism doth also now save us; not the putting away of the filth of the flesh, but the answer of a good conscience towards God." The word baptism signifies immersion, and that we are so to understand it in this place appears from the natural and incidental effect here mentioned, namely, the putting away of the filth of the flesh. This the apostle disclaims, but it is immersion which suggested and needed the disclaimer: sprinkling could not have suggested the negative remark. The meaning of the word, and the history of baptism, both teach immersion; and the doctrine receives confirmation from such texts as the one before us.

There is a peculiarity in this text which renders each of these remarks more emphatic. I refer to the general or comprehensive mode in which the truth is expressed in 1 Pet. iii. 21.* He speaks of "*baptism*" and of "*us*" as though it were one and the same in every case. Apply this peculiarity to the qualifications of the baptized, and it teaches us that every one must have the same qualifications; there is no exception of infants, or of anyone else. It is baptism in every instance; the nature of the ordinance is always the same; and the answer of a good conscience is universally required. The same principle is recognized in Rom. vi. 4, and in Gal. iii. 27: and all of them exclude the distinction between infants and adults. THERE IS BUT ONE BAPTISM —THE BAPTISM OF BELIEVERS.

---

* Baptism is here called the antitype of the preservation of Noah in the ark. The water which overwhelmed the world bore up the ark; so death, which is the destruction of the world, is the salvation of the believer, for by death Christ destroyed him that had the power of death, that is, the devil. Now, as many as are baptized into Christ, are baptized into his death, being buried with him by baptism into death, (Rom. vi. 3, 4); and "if we have been planted together in the likeness of his death, we shall be also in the likeness of his resurrection": ver. 5.—J. H.

A Biographical Sketch of William Shirreff (1792-1832)

BY

JOHN FRANKLIN JONES

A Biographical Sketch of William Shirreff (1792-1832)

William Shirreff was born in 1762 at Coldstream, Berwickshire, Scotland. An only child, he received a good education and was disposed to excellence in his educational efforts and in life (Spurgeon, xv).

He received frequent childhood religious impressions regarding his religious state. Particularly at age twelve or thirteen, he was impressed via his parents reading of the Puritans (Ibid., xv). He took his first communion in the Scotch Established Church at age sixteen, but noted in his diary his relapsed spiritual state (Ibid., xv).

His spiritual impressions returned at age seventeen after the death of his father. He removed to Edinburgh and entered a lengthy course of study at the University. An excellent Greek, Hebrew, and Latin scholar, proficient in modern languages, he studied mathematics and the other branches of learning, being most interested in the study of theology (Ibid., xvi).

The congregation of the St. Ninians, Stirling parish, called him to be their pastor when he was twenty-six. They paid to the patron a substantial sum of money to secure his appointment to them (Ibid., xvi). His daily habit was to rise early, walk, spend lengthy periods in prayer, study, visit, and close the day reading a worthy book to, or instructing from Scripture, his family (Ibid., xxi).

He wrote out, but never read, his sermons. He especially enjoyed reading the older divines. Particularly fond of Edwards, he often quoted his words: "Resolved, to serve God, though no one else should do so" (Ibid., xxv). Haldane ranked him among the most "learned, popular, and impressive preachers in the Church of Scotland." He devoted himself to study and amassed a large personal library (Ibid., xvi).

He taught a large Bible class at St. Ninians which included persons above fifteen and large numbers of married persons. He regularly used the larger catechism as the main textbook for the class (Ibid., xxv).

Because St. Ninians was so large, he often held meetings at various points around the parish (xxiv). He was warmly evangelistic, often recording in his diary encounters of usefulness to bringing sinners to conviction and conversion (Ibid., xxv).

With time, his studies brought him to the error of uniting Church and State, and especially, to the errors associated with the practice of baptism.(xvii). He examined and collated all the biblical passages related to the Greek word for baptizo. He read all the classical authors to which he had access. He came to the place that he rejected infant sprinkling and embraced believers' baptism (Ibid., xxvi).

He resigned his charge at St. Ninians and the Presbytery of Stirling, a position he held for thirty- five years (Ibid., xvii). He took as his text Acts 20:32 when he preached his final sermon to his people at St. Ninians (Ibid., xxvii).

Dr. Innes baptized Shirreff in Edinburgh in 1823. He intended to settle at Edinburgh, but was called by the congregation of the Baptist Church, Albion Street, Glasgow, to be their pastor. He labored among that congregation for nine years (Ibid., xvii).

He composed and delivered a series of lectures designed to explain to his former congregation and former Presbytery his new views on baptism and how he came to them. Shortly after he settled in Albion Street Chapel, he delivered them in a weekly series of sermons. Though he exhibited no intention to publish them, J. A. Haldane published them after Shirreff's death (Ibid., xix).

In 1804, he married Mary Russell (Ibid., xx), daughter of the minister at Stirling (Ibid., xxi). He kept a diary till the end of his life, but from 1796 wrote same in his self-devised shorthand. Though he taught his system to his sons, many of the entries were illegible even to them (Ibid., xxv).

He continued to preach, despite his failing health, to within five weeks of his death. The day before his death, he said to Mrs. Shirreff, "Who are these? What fine singing!" Though she told him no one was present but the two of them, he said, as he pointed to the top of the bed, "They are there. What fine singing!" (Ibid., xxxi). He died at nine the next morning (Ibid., xxxii), ca. 1832, just short of seventy years old (Ibid., xxxxii).

BIBLIORGAPHY

Spurgeon, Charles Haddon. "Prefatory Memoir" to *Lectures on Baptism*, by William Shirreff. London: Passmore and Alabaster, 1878; reprinted, Paris, AR: Baptist Standard Bearer, 1987.

Starr, Edward C., ed. *A Baptist Bibliography Being a Register of Printed Material By and About Baptists; Including Works Written Against the Baptists*. S.v. "Shirreff, William (1762-1832)."

BY JOHN FRANKLIN JONES
CORDOVA, TENNESSEE
JULY 2006

THE BAPTIST STANDARD BEARER, INC.

a non-profit, tax-exempt corporation
committed to the Publication & Preservation
of the Baptist Heritage.

CURRENT TITLES AVAILABLE IN
THE BAPTIST *DISTINCTIVES* SERIES

KIFFIN, WILLIAM — A Sober Discourse of Right to Church-Communion. Wherein is proved by Scripture, the Example of the Primitive Times, and the Practice of All that have Professed the Christian Religion: That no Unbaptized person may be Regularly admitted to the Lord's Supper. (London: George Larkin, 1681).

KINGHORN, JOSEPH — Baptism, A Term of Communion. (Norwich: Bacon, Kinnebrook, and Co., 1816)

KINGHORN, JOSEPH — A Defense of "Baptism, A Term of Communion". In Answer To Robert Hall's Reply. (Norwich: Wilkin and Youngman, 1820).

GILL, JOHN — Gospel Baptism. A Collection of Sermons, Tracts, etc., on Scriptural Authority, the Nature of the New Testament Church and the Ordinance of Baptism by John Gill. (Paris, AR: The Baptist Standard Bearer, Inc., 2006).

CARSON, ALEXANDER	Ecclesiastical Polity of the New Testament. (Dublin: William Carson, 1856).
BOOTH, ABRAHAM	A Defense of the Baptists. A Declaration and Vindication of Three Historically Distinctive Baptist Principles. Compiled and Set Forth in the Republication of Three Books. Revised edition. (Paris, AR: The Baptist Standard Bearer, Inc., 2006).
BOOTH, ABRAHAM	Paedobaptism Examined on the Principles, Concessions, and Reasonings of the Most Learned Paedobaptists. With Replies to the Arguments and Objections of Dr. Williams and Mr. Peter Edwards. 3 volumes. (London: Ebenezer Palmer, 1829).
CARROLL, B. H.	*Ecclesia* - The Church. With an Appendix. (Louisville: Baptist Book Concern, 1903).
CHRISTIAN, JOHN T.	Immersion, The Act of Christian Baptism. (Louisville: Baptist Book Concern, 1891).
FROST, J. M.	Pedobaptism: Is It From Heaven Or Of Men? (Philadelphia: American Baptist Publication Society, 1875).
FULLER, RICHARD	Baptism, and the Terms of Communion; An Argument. (Charleston, SC: Southern Baptist Publication Society, 1854).
GRAVES, J. R.	Tri-Lemma: or, Death By Three Horns. The Presbyterian General Assembly Not Able To Decide This Question: "Is Baptism In The Romish Church Valid?" 1st Edition.

	(Nashville: Southwestern Publishing House, 1861).
MELL, P.H.	Baptism In Its Mode and Subjects. (Charleston, SC: Southern Baptist Publications Society, 1853).
JETER, JEREMIAH B.	Baptist Principles Reset. Consisting of Articles on Distinctive Baptist Principles by Various Authors. With an Appendix. (Richmond: The Religious Herald Co., 1902).
PENDLETON, J.M.	Distinctive Principles of Baptists. (Philadelphia: American Baptist Publication Society, 1882).
THOMAS, JESSE B.	The Church and the Kingdom. A New Testament Study. (Louisville: Baptist Book Concern, 1914).
WALLER, JOHN L.	Open Communion Shown to be Unscriptural & Deleterious. With an introductory essay by Dr. D. R. Campbell and an Appendix. (Louisville: Baptist Book Concern, 1859).

For a complete list of current authors/titles, visit our internet site at:
www.standardbearer.org
or write us at:

he Baptist Standard Bearer, Inc.

NUMBER ONE IRON OAKS DRIVE • PARIS, ARKANSAS 72855

TEL # 479-963-3831   *FAX # 479-963-8083*
EMAIL: Baptist@centurytel.net   *http://www.standardbearer.org*

Thou hast given a standard to them that fear thee; that it may be displayed because of the truth. — Psalm 60:4